Ferrari

Larry Edsall

Photography by Dennis Adler

motorbooks

First published in 2011 by Motorbooks, an imprint of MBI Publishing Company, 400 First Avenue North, Suite 300, Minneapolis, MN 55401 USA

Motorbooks titles are also available at discounts in bulk quantity for industrial or sales-promotional use. For details write to Special Sales Manager at MBI Publishing Company, 400 First Avenue North, Suite 300, Minneapolis, MN 55401 USA.

To find out more about our books, visit us online at www.motorbooks.com.

Library of Congress Cataloging-in-Publication Data

Edsall, Larry.
  Ferrari / Larry Edsall ; photographs by Dennis Adler.
    p. cm.
  Includes index.
  ISBN 978-0-7603-4058-5 (sb w/ flaps)
  1. Ferrari automobile—History. 2. Ferrari automobile—History—Pictorial works. 3. Ferrari, Enzo, 1898-1988. I. Adler, Dennis, 1948- ill. II. Title.
  TL215.F47E37 2011
  629.222'2—dc22
                            2011010555

Editors: Carmen Nickisch and Darwin Holmstrom
Design Manager: Kou Lor
Layout by: Kazuko Collins

Printed in China

On the front cover: TR250 Testa Rossa
On the back cover: 1974 Dino GTS
On the frontis: 1981 512 Berlinetta Boxer
On the title page: 212 Inter

CONTENTS

INTRODUCTION

Ironic, isn't it, that Ferraris have become the most cherished of all automobiles, because the truth is that Enzo Ferrari didn't want to build cars that people would drive on city streets and country roads or that valets would park right up front at the fanciest of restaurants. All Enzo Ferrari wanted to do was to build cars that would compete—that is, win—on racetracks. He built those cars for his own team of drivers, though to cover the cost of such activities, he built some that he sold to others who shared his passion for the race to the finish line.

Ferrari discovered that there was even more demand for cars he built primarily for everyday driving, and here we are, more than a century beyond his birth and more than two decades since his death at the age of 90, and Ferrari's latest cars, few though they may be, are eagerly purchased by the well-to-do. Those of older vintage frequently command seven figures—sometimes even eight—at collector car auctions around the world.

In fact, one major classic car auction company executive, whose livelihood depends on paying particularly close attention to such things, has revealed that while Ferraris comprise only a small percentage of the collector cars sold at auctions each year, they account for nearly half of the money spent by bidders at those events.

Such is the mystique of the cars that bear Enzo Ferrari's last name and the prancing horse emblem he chose to place on them.

Ah, the prancing horse. Ferrari's emblem was inspired by a similar insignia used by Francesco Baracca, Italian flying ace in World War I. Baracca had been a member of the Piedmont Calvary, and the rampant horse was on the planes he flew. When Ferrari was a young racing car driver, he met Baracca's parents, who were from Lugo, a hometown they shared with Ferrari's own mother, who was the daughter of a wealthy farm family. Countess Baracca noticed Ferrari's interest in an old airplane bearing her son's emblem, and she suggested it would be a good-luck charm for Ferrari to use it on his racing cars.

Good luck, indeed. Ferrari's cars have had a charmed life, it seems, from the beginning.

Enzo Ferrari was born on February 18, 1898, at Modena in northern Italy, where his father produced metal components for bridges and other structures. Ferrari was in his late teens when his father and older brother died during a flu epidemic on the eve of World War I. When Enzo returned from service with the Italian army, he found the company in failure. He moved to Torino (Turin) seeking employment.

When Enzo was a child, his father had taken him to see auto races, igniting an early passion for fast cars and motor sports. His other passions were opera—at one point he dreamed of becoming a famous singer—and writing, especially about sports, which he did for a local newspaper as a teenager. In Turin, Ferrari worked for a several small automotive businesses but eventually became a mechanic, then a test driver, race car drive (in 11 seasons, he drove in 38 races and won 9 of them), racing team manager, marketing manager, and eventually a regional agent for Alfa Romeo.

Ferrari left Alfa Romeo and started his own company, Auto-Avio Costruzioni, to build components he would sell to various racing teams. But what he wanted was his own team, which he established after World War II as Scuderia (the Italian word for *stable* or *team*) Ferrari.

Although his Auto-Avio Costruzioni had built two sports cars from Fiat parts and entered them in the Mille Miglia/Grand Prix of Brescia in 1940, the first car to bear Ferrari's name was the 125 S, a racing roadster powered by a V12 twin-six engine.

If the creation of such a complicated powerplant seems a huge task for a fledgling company, understand how driven Ferrari was to build the best and fastest cars. As he wrote in one of his autobiographies, "I have always loved V12 twin-six engines, ever since I saw photographs of the first V12 twin-six Packard at Indianapolis back in 1914 and the Delage that came in second at Lyons in 1924. I have always loved the sound of the engine. . . ."

Ah, the sound of the engine, especially the V12, especially the Ferrari V12. It's a sound so many of us have come to love, including the author's youngest daughter, Abby, who loved the Ferraris her father sometimes would drive home when he was an editor at *AutoWeek* magazine. At the end of each summer, Abby would come along eagerly to the big collector car auction at Auburn, Indiana, where she could see not just one Ferrari, but a handful or even a dozen or more of them as they awaited their turn to be driven across the auction block.

This book is part of a "First Gear" series, meant to introduce the passion for automobiles to another generation. Enzo Ferrari had that passion, from an early age, and the cars bearing his name and the prancing horse emblem that emitted that wonderful exhaust note have ignited the emotions of Abby and millions more around the globe.

Ferrari may not have become an opera singer, but his cars certainly have provided us with a wonderful symphony of sound.

In addition to personal experience with Ferraris, interviews with people such as Sergio and Andrea Pininfarina, and research for his earlier books—*Concept Cars, Legendary Cars,* and *Masters of Car Design*—the author drew from the following sources in the preparation of this text:

Ferrari: A Complete Guide to All Models, by Leonardo Acerbi, Motorbooks, 2005

Standard Catalog of Ferrari 1947–2003, by Mike Covello, Krause Publication, 2003

The Ferrari Phenomenon, by Matt Stone and Luca Dal Monte, David Bull Publishing, 2010

Ferrari: Design of a Legend: The Official History and Catalog, Abbeville Press, 1990

CAR MEN #3: Sergio Pininfarina: Pininfarina Studi & Ricerche, by Riccardo P. Felicioli, Automobilia, 1998

CHAPTER 1
RACERS FOR THE ROAD

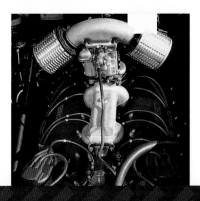

In the United States, auto racing—whether it involved open-wheel, Indianapolis-type cars, or fully fendered, stock-style sedans—primarily evolved on racetracks called "ovals," although they actually comprised two parallel straightaways, linked at either end by an arch-like curve. That wasn't the case in Europe, where what we have come to know as "road racing" was the primary pursuit for those with the need for speed.

European road racing was just that: Racing on public roads, albeit roads that in most cases had been closed to regular traffic. Certainly, there were closed circuits that, like the oval tracks in the United States, had been designed especially for high-speed competition, but just like regular roads, these circuits included a variety of turns—to the left and to the right—as well as changes in elevation.

Instead of American-style Indy cars or big Detroit-built sedans, Europeans primarily raced what we now know as "sports cars," two-seaters that were either open-cockpit roadsters or hard-roofed coupes. Such cars could be driven on public roads during the week and raced on those same roads, or on specially created road courses, on weekends.

It was for such competition that Enzo Ferrari and his team built their earliest cars. But even then, some of those cars were built to satisfy customers who were more interested in daily driving than weekend racing.

In 1939, when Enzo Ferrari left Alfa Romeo, where he ran the racing team, he took with him people such as engineers Giuseppe Busso and Gioachino Colombo and test driver Luigi Bazzi. Ferrari agreed not to race for four years, and it wasn't until World War II was over that he really had the opportunity to start building the cars that would bear his name.

The first was the 125 S, launched early in 1947. The two-seat roadster was designed by Colombo and was built around a 1.5-liter "twin-six" V12 powerplant ready for supercharging and potential entry into Grand Prix racing. Credit for this engine goes to Busso, not Colombo.

The car was the first to wear the prancing black horse against a yellow background with Italy's colors above and Ferrari's *F* beneath.

The 125 S made its racing debut in May with driver Franco Cortese battling with Maserati

6CS 1500s throughout the event at Piacenza. Cortese was leading with only three laps to go when the car's fuel pump failed, and Cortese did not finish the race. But he and the car did win two weeks later in the Grand Prix of Rome. By the end of the season, the 125 S and 125 S Corsa had won 7 of their 14 starts.

Cortese was not a professional racer, but a salesman who sold machine tools produced by Ferrari.

FERRARI TIPO 125 S

Year produced: 1947
Number produced: 2
Price: Not available
Engine (displacement/horsepower): 1.5-liter V12/118 horsepower
0–60 miles per hour: Not available
Top speed: 105 miles per hour

Did You Know?

The first cars actually built by Enzo Ferrari were a pair of eight-cylinder Auto-Avio Costruzioni 815 roadsters created in 1940 from Fiat components. Touring designed low-slung bodywork for the cars, which competed in the 1940 Mille Miglia race with the likes of Alberto Ascari and Enrico Nardi behind the steering wheels.

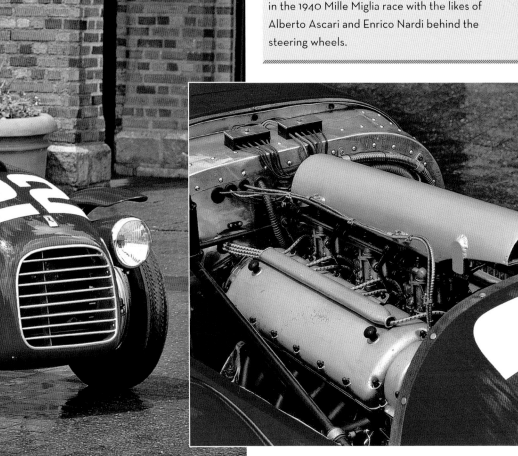

Phil Hill
D. Sydorick

Launched in 1948, Ferrari's 166 model was an evolution of the 125 S and was produced in a variety of forms and with bodywork supplied by the likes of Vignale, Allemano, Bertone, Ghia, and Pinin Farina and Stabilimenti Farina, among others. All, however, shared versions of the new 2.0-liter V12 engine designed by Gioachino Colombo.

There were single-seaters: the 166 F2 wearing three carburetors for the new Formula Two racing series, and the 166 S with a single carburetor for Sport category racing.

There were two-seat, single-carb cars: the 166 SC (Spyder Corsa) with motorcycle-style

166 MILLE MIGLIA, SPYDER CORSA

Years produced: 1948–1951
Number produced: 166 S: 2
  166 MM: 32
  166 Inter: 37
Price: Not available
Engine (displacement/horsepower):
  2.0-liter V12/130–155 horsepower with three carburetors
  2.0-liter v12/110 horsepower with one carburetor
0–60 miles per hour: Not available
Top speed: 135 miles per hour (166 MM Touring)

fenders, the 166 S Allemano (as open roadster or closed coupe), and the 166 MM Zagato (with coupe bodywork by Zagato). There were two-seat, three-carb cars: the 166 MM Touring, which took its name from its roadster body by Touring. The car made its debut in the fall at the 1948 Turin Motor Show.

And there were the Ferrari 166 Inter models, introduced late in the year at the Paris show as a Touring-bodied coupe, though eventually available with roadster, coupe, and convertible styling from various *carrozzieri* and with single or triple carburetors.

The 166 S made its debut with Clemente Biondetti driving it to victory in the Targa Florio. A month later, and now with Allemano coupe bodywork, Biondetti won again in the Mille Miglia, co-driving with Giuseppe Navone and winning by nearly an hour and a half. However, the star of that race was Tazio Nuvolari, who, though ill, had driven magnificently through the field and built a lead of 29 minutes, only to have his race end because of a broken spring.

Did You Know?

The 166 F2 made quite a debut: Raymond Sommers drove the car to victory in the Grand Prix of Florence, not only leading from the start but lapping the entire field.

166 MILLE MIGLIA, SPYDER CORSA

For the 1949 Geneva Motor Show, Stabilimenti Farina showed its spin on the Ferrari 166 MM.

In 1948, Ferrari had produced two versions of the 166 MM, a coup and an open, topless roadster. At Geneva, Stabilimenti Farina equipped the Spyder with a convertible top.

Stabilimenti Farina was founded by Giovanni Farina and had one of the first stamping presses used to make metal car body parts in Italy. Among Giovanni's employees were his younger brothers Carlo and Battista, who was better known by his nickname, Pinin, and who left Stabilimenti Farina in 1928 to start his own more design-oriented shop.

Stabilimenti Farina did pioneering work on such features as hydraulic brakes and shocks and convertible tops, and it employed designers Pietro Frua, Mario Boano, Mario Revelli de Beaumont, Alfredo Vignale, and Giovanni Michelotti.

While Enzo Ferrari thought the convertible top bastardized the design of his open roadster, Ferrari racing driver and American importer Luigi Chinetti realized the feature would enhance the cars' sales potential.

It certainly worked on the 011S chassis. After the Geneva show, the car was purchased by famed Italian movie director Roberto Rossellini.

011S

Year produced: 1949
Number produced: Stabilimenti Farina built bodies for only nine Ferrari 166s, three of them convertibles
Price: Not available
Engine (displacement/horsepower): 2.0-liter V12/110 horsepower
0–60 miles per hour: Not available
Top speed: 135 miles per hour

Did You Know?

Giovanni Farina's son, Giuseppe, who was best known by his nickname, Nino, won the first World Driving Championship in 1950 while racing for the Alfa Romeo team.

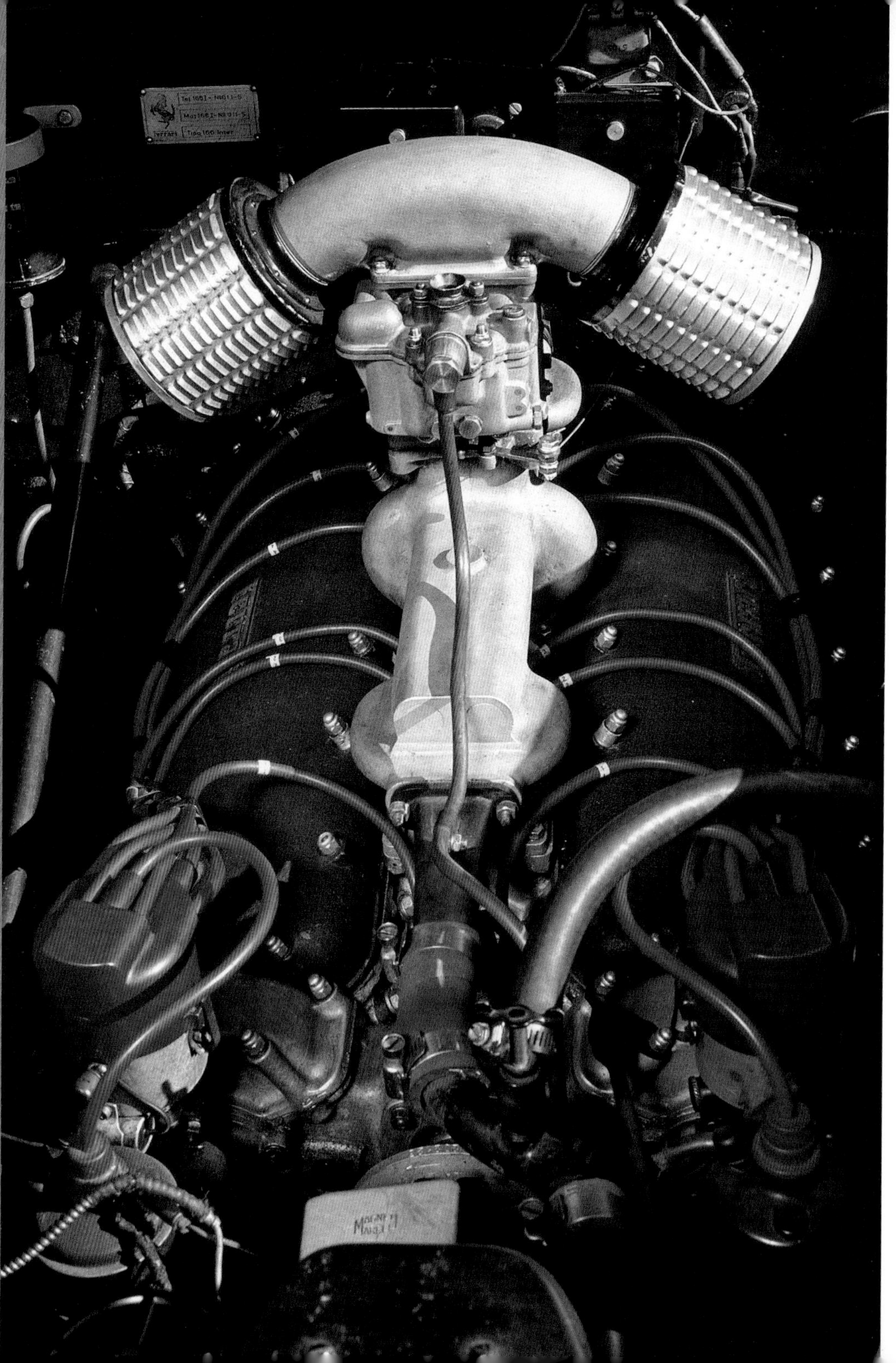

The Ferrari 212 Inter was a grand touring car that debuted at the 1951 Paris Motor Show with bodywork by Vignale. The car was similar to the previous 195 model, but rode a wheelbase that had been stretched from 82 to 85 inches and used a bored version of the same V12 engine, enlarged to 2,562cc. Eventually, the engine's single carburetor would give way to a trio of units, resulting in an increase from 155 to 170 horsepower.

After the original Vignale-bodied car was shown at Paris, others designed and produced their own coachwork, including Ghia, which created both a 2+2 coupe and a four-seat sedan, something new for Ferrari.

Though it was called the 212 Export, this version wasn't designed for sales outside Italy but for racing. The 212 Export got aggressive bodywork from Vignale. Though raced as a coupe, the 212 Export

was unveiled at the 1951 Geneva show as a convertible.

Some of the Export designs seemed whimsical, but they were effective on the racetrack. Carrozzeria Fontana created special bodywork for the Marzotto brothers. Vittorio Marzotto won the 1951 Giro di Sicilia in his so-called Sicilian cart, while Giannio Marzotto drove into the lead in the Mille Miglia in the very rounded "Marzotto's Egg."

212 INTER

Years produced: 1951–1953
Number produced: 125 (including some 25 Export versions)
Price: $9,500
Engine (displacement/horsepower): 2,562cc/155–170 horsepower
0–60 miles per hour: Not available
Top speed: 180 miles per hour

Did You Know?

The now long-standing relationship between Ferrari and Pinin Farina started with two 1952 212 Inter convertibles, including one in metallic silver that was displayed at the 1952 Paris Motor Show.

The 225 S (S for Sport) was Ferrari's factory sports car racer for the 1952 season. Its significance extended beyond the track, however, because its styling—especially the three porthole vents trailing the front wheelwells—established cues that would become Ferrari trademarks.

The car used the latest developments in Ferrari's V12 engine progression, starting with a 2.7-liter version. The car made its competitive debut in the Giro di Sicilia in the form of an open roadster and a closed coupe, both with bodywork by Vignale.

225 S

Year produced: 1952
Number produced: 7
Price: Not available
Engine (displacement/horsepower): 2.7-liter V12/210 horsepower
0-60 miles per hour: Not available
Top speed: 140 miles per hour

By the Mille Miglia, Ferrari had fielded seven 225 S cars.

The car's first major victory came in the Grand Prix of Monaco, which in 1952 was contested not by Grand Prix racers but by sports cars, with Italian aristocrat Vittorio Marzotto winning in a Vignale 225 S Barchetta.

Ferrari's V12 engine development reached a milestone with a 3.0-liter version, and the 225 gave way to a hugely significant new model—the 250.

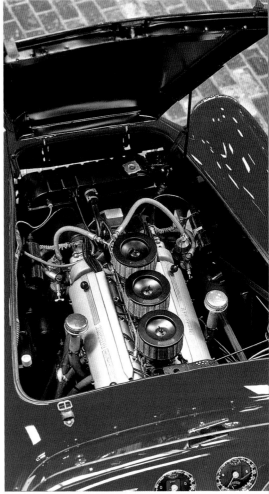

225 S

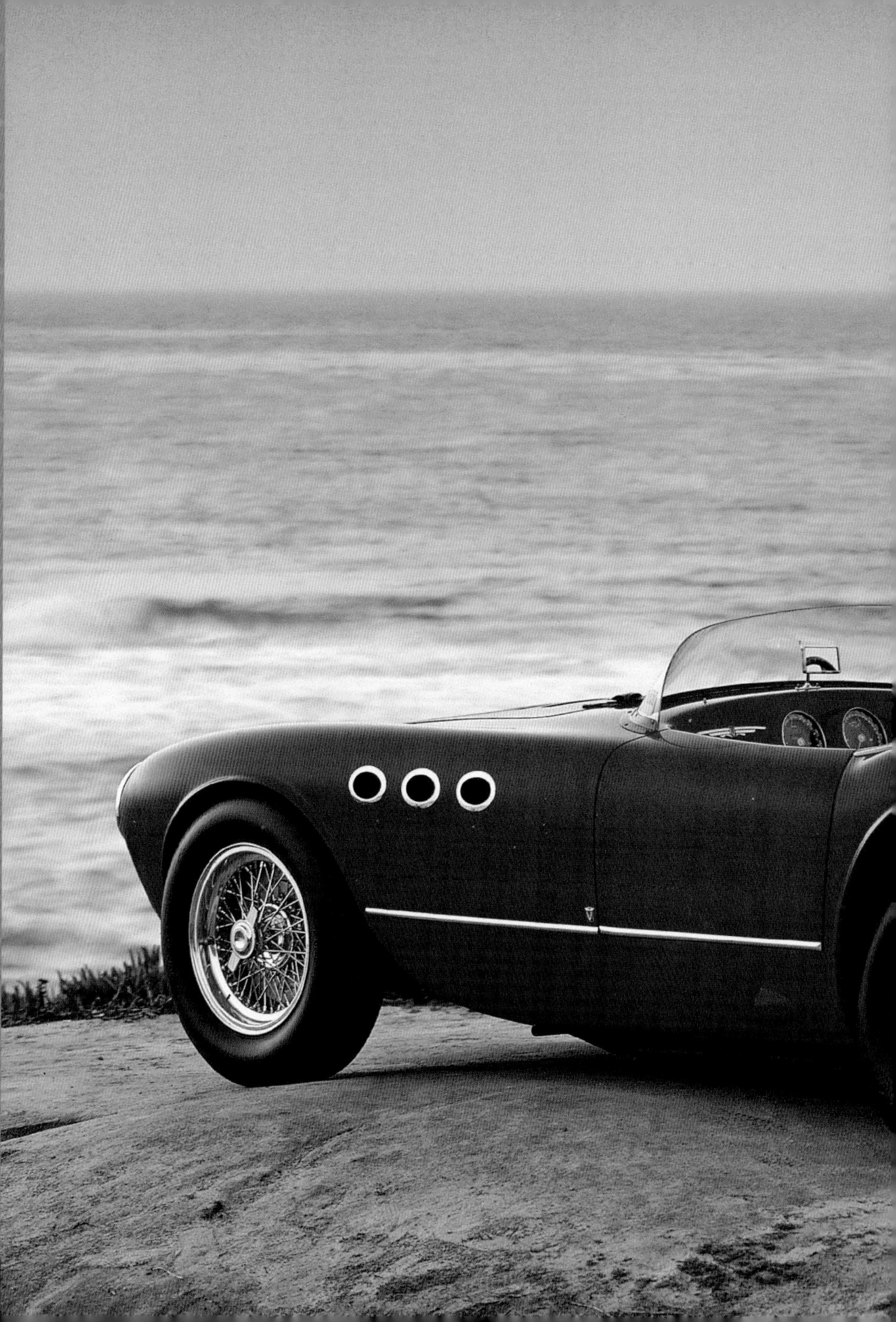

In 1951 and 1952, Ferrari's 500 F2 won 14 of 15 races in the hands of Alberto Ascari, Mike Hawthorn, and Piero Taruffi. But in 1953, the rules changed and instead of a 2-liter limit, the regulation was raised to 2.5 liters. Rather than abandon Aurelio Lampredi's marvelous little motor, Ferrari took it from open wheel to sports-car racing.

The 500 Mondial (*Mondial* means "world" in Italian) was named in honor of Ascari's recent world driving championships. Ascari and Gigi Villoresi drove in the car's debut in late December 1953 in the 12-hour race at Casablanca.

While the engine was borrowed from the Formula car, it ran in the sports car in slightly detuned tuning. In the F2, it employed four carburetors, had up to 13:1 compression, and delivered as much as 185 horsepower. For sports car racing, the engine had a pair of Webers, 9.2:1 compression, and a still impressive 170 horsepower.

Though overpowered by V12 rivals, including Ferrari's own 375 MM that won at Casablanca, the 500 Mondial went on to a successful career. With its light weight—the 500 Mondial weighed less than 1,600 pounds—and deft handling, it could compete with more-powerful competitors, as demonstrated in the 1954 Mille Miglia, where Vittorio Marzotto finished in second place.

500 MONDIAL

Years produced: 1953–1954
Number produced: Not available
Price: Not available
Engine (displacement / horsepower): 2.0-liter four-cylinder/170 horsepower
0–60 miles per hour: Not available
Top speed: 150 miles per hour

Did You Know?

The first 500 Mondial was the very first Ferrari constructed by carrozzeria Scaglietti, which would go on to build many of Ferrari's sports-racing cars in the coming years.

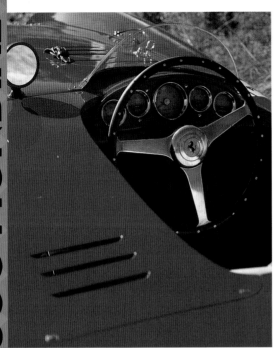

In 1956, Ferrari used the auto show at Brussels to unveil its new 410 Superamerica model. Later that year, at the Paris show, Ferrari showed the car's true potential in the form of the Superfast concept car.

To create the Superfast version, Pinin Farina shortened the car's chassis to enhance its proportions, then wrapped it in bodywork that took the Superamerica cues to the extreme.

The nose was elongated, with a lowered grille and angled headlamps. The vents behind the front wheelwells were more dramatic. The top section of the rear wheelwells was filled in. Instead of a wraparound rear window, the panels behind the front windows matched the bodywork.

The car's appearance was accentuated by a dramatic two-tone paint scheme of white over a satin-finished dark gray.

And yet Pinin Farina was just getting started!

The two most dramatic elements of the car were

• Its large tail fins. They encompassed the entire rear quarter panels, rising ahead of

the rear wheels and sweeping back, up and out over triangular taillamps.

- Its pillar-less windshield. Instead of the traditional A pillars, the windshield angled back to the side windows.

The car not only looked super fast, it was. Road tests discovered its triple-carbureted V12 powered it from a standing start to 60 miles per hour in just 5.6 seconds, and it reached a top speed of 160 miles per hour (or even slightly faster).

SUPERFAST I

Year produced: 1956 concept car
Number produced: 1
Price: $18,500
Engine (displacement/horsepower): 5.0-liter V12/380 horsepower
0–60 miles per hour: 5.6 seconds
Top speed: 160 miles per hour

Did You Know?

Because the automotive design by Battista "Pinin" Farina and his family became so well known, and known by people around the world as simply "Pininfarina," the president of Italy signed a decree in 1961 officially changing the family's name to Pininfarina.

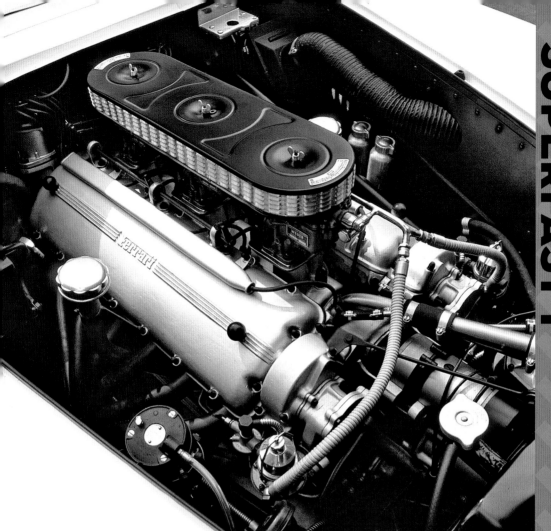

In 1956, two of Enzo Ferrari's best customers came to him with a special request: They wanted to buy Ferrari 250 GTs, but instead of bodywork by the usual suspects—Touring, Ghia, Pinin Farina—they wanted their cars done by Ugo Zagato and his sons and their carrozzeria.

Ugo Zagato had been involved in aircraft construction during World War I and after the war applied what he learned to automobile body design. His cars were light and aerodynamic and often featured a "double-bubble" roof that allowed room for helmeted occupants while lowering the roof's center section to reduce wind resistance.

Vladimiro Galluzzi wanted his Zagato-bodied Ferrari for use both on the road and on the racetrack, while Camillo Luglio was interested only in his car's capability as a racer. Thus, while the cars were similar in design, they differed in some details. For example, Galluzzi's had a Lancia blue body with white roof while Galluzzi's was sheetmetal gray and lacked anything that might be considered a frill that would add unwanted weight on the track.

Luglio won the 1956 Italian sports car championship in his car while Galluzzi's car not only competed on the track but won honors at concours d'elegance.

The cars' successes caused three more to be commissioned. After winning his racing championship, Luglio sold his car and ordered another for the 1957 season. Luglio again won the national championship and showed up for the Mille Miglia with sponsorship from the Idriz paint company, which became one of the first companies to pay to put its name on a racing car.

Vittorio de Micheli also ordered an example, with a less powerful but still competitive engine.

Like Luglio, Galluzzi also ordered a second car, though this time for the road, not for racing, and without the double-bubble top but with two tail fins.

1956 250 GTZ TDF

Years produced: 1956–1957
Number produced: 5
Price: Not available
Engine (displacement/horsepower): 2.5-liter V12/240 horsepower
0–60 miles per hour: Not available
Top speed: Not available

Did You Know?

The GTZ wasn't the first Ferrari bodied by Zagato. In 1949, Ugo Zagato created the so-called Panoramica roof for a Ferrari 166 Mille Miglia owned by auto racer and Piaggio scooter dealer Antonio Stagnoli. In the winter of 1952–1953, Luigi Bosisio of Milan had Zagato take a 166 MM with a barchetta body by Touring and transform it into the Elaborata coupe.

1956 250 GTZ TDF

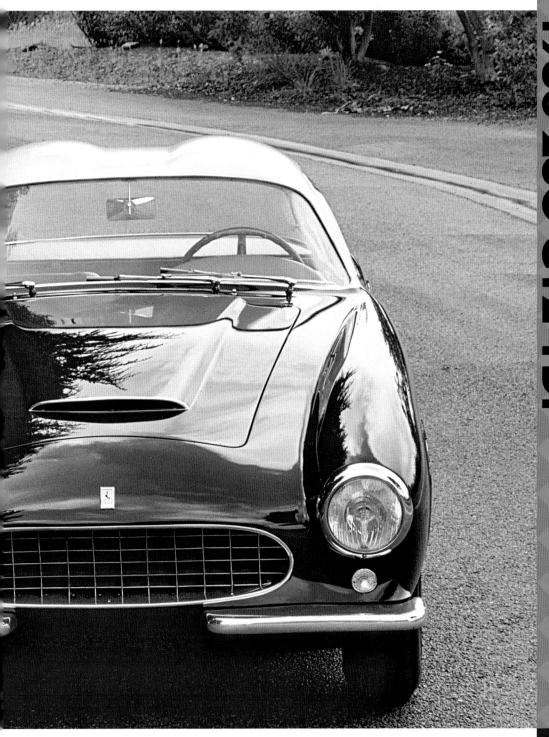

CHAPTER 2

OF ROADS, RACERS AND REDHEADS

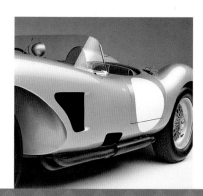

Though this book focuses primarily on cars built for the road, Ferrari remained devoted to auto racing and pursued both open-wheel, Grand Prix competition as well as sports car competition at events such as the 24 Hours of Le Mans. It won Le Mans in 1949—the first post-war resumption of a race rivaled only by the Indianapolis 500 in historic legend—and then again in 1954.

But by the mid-1950s, Ferrari needed to update and upgrade if it was to remain competitive on the track (and on the road) against the likes of Mercedes-Benz, Porsche, Jaguar, and Maserati. A key element in that update was a new, larger but lighter and more powerful 3.0-liter V12 engine, an engine that was used in a series of sports cars that were successful on the racetrack and gorgeous on the road and that today have become among the most cherished by car collectors.

Those cars were the 250s, and they ranged from Pinin Farina–designed 250 GT sports cars to the 250 TR (redhead) racer that in 1958 put Ferrari back into the winner's circle at Le Mans, a location that become something of a Prancing Horse stable, with Ferrari also winning races from 1960 through 1965.

In 1951, Ferrari fielded its first car with the word *America* in its name—the 340 America, a black coupe with dark green leather interior, intended to appeal to Americans for sports car racing. Later that year came the 342 America, the grand touring version of the car—a coupe with bodywork by Ghia. But it was an elegant convertible by Pinin Farina that made this model truly appealing. The *America* label was used again in 1953 on the 375 America.

Then, in 1956, Ferrari took the *America* theme a giant step forward with the 410 Superamerica, which was built on a new Ferrari chassis and powered by a 5.0-liter V12 that became more powerful as the years progressed, finally reaching 400 horsepower in its Series III form.

The Superamerica was unveiled at the Brussels Motor Show with elegant coupe bodywork by Pinin Farina, highlighted by large air vents behind the front wheels and subtle tail fins.

For the Paris show that fall, Ferrari unveiled a second version of the 410, the 410 Superfast. Built on a slightly shortened chassis, the Superfast featured dramatic styling, with Pinin Farina devising a unique greenhouse with no A pillars, a large backlight but huge wedge-shaped B pillars, and large and sharply creased tail fins flying over small rear bumper bars.

410 SUPERAMERICA

Years produced: 1956–1959
Number produced: 36
Price: $16,800 (Superamerica), $18,500 (Superfast)
Engine (displacement/horsepower): 5.0-liter V12/340–400 horsepower
0–60 miles per hour: Not available
Top speed: 165 miles per hour

Did You Know?

Though the target market for the Ferrari 342 America was obvious from the car's name, one of the first buyers was Leopold, the former king of Belgium.

After winning the Tour de France races from 1956 to 1959, the Ferrari 250 GT Berlinetta became better known as the GT Tour de France (Ferrari went on to extend its Tour de France winning streak through 1964).

Originally built as the 250 GT Competizione, the idea behind the Tour de France (TdF) cars was to produce a more aggressive version of the 250 Europe and 250 GT coupes for owners intent on motorsports competition.

Ferrari had Scaglietti build 10 such cars for 1956 (well, actually 8, with the other 2 done, at customers' requests, by Zagato), a dozen more early in 1957 with slightly refined bodywork, including 14 vents behind the front wheels and a smaller rear window, and then 15 more later in the year with covered headlights and three-vent front fenders.

In 1958, 29 Tour de France cars were built, now with large fender vents. Finally, in 1959, Pininfarina built 7 more "Interim" cars using

the same chassis, but the prototype bodywork was designed for the 250 GT SWB Berlinetta.

The long-wheelbase cars were powered by Ferrari's 3.0-liter V12 engine, which in various years and guises provided at least 240 and as much as 260 horsepower.

In addition to its victories in the Tour de France road race and various hillclimbs, the 250 GT Tour de France won the 1957 Mille Miglia.

250 GT TDF

Years produced: 1956–1959
Number produced: 73
Price: $11,000
Engine (displacement/horsepower): 3.0-liter V12/240–260 horsepower
0–60 miles per hour: 6.9 seconds
Top speed: 135 miles per hour

Did You Know?

Luigi Chinetti drove a Ferrari 166 MM Touring to victory in the 12 Hours of Paris race in 1948. A year later, he was behind the steering wheel for 23 of the 24 hours at Le Mans, where his 166 MM Touring again was the first across the finish line. The car also won the 24-hour race at Spa that year. Though a successful racer, Chinetti would really make his name as Ferrari's importer for North America.

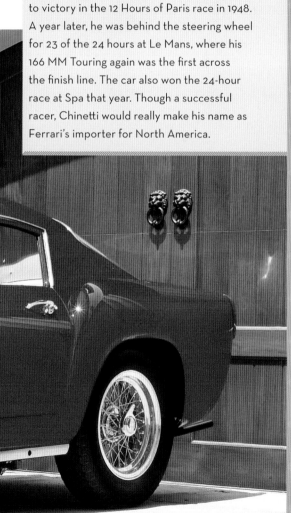

After horrific crashes that killed spectators at Le Mans in 1955 and at the Mille Miglia in 1957, Enzo Ferrari knew that new rules would be drafted to make sports car racing safer for competitors and fans alike, and those rules would mean changes for the cars themselves.

Anticipating those changes, including rules that would reduce engine displacement, Ferrari's shop went to work on a new sports racer. The prototype for this new car made its debut at the Nürburgring race in 1957 and proved its capability by posting the sixth-fastest time despite the size of its engine.

By Le Mans, a pair of the new cars, though still only prototypes, wore stunning bodywork designed by Sergio Scaglietti, whose automotive repair and coachbuilding business was across the road from Ferrari. The sports-car bodywork

250 TESTA ROSSA

Years produced: 1956–1961
Number produced: 34
Price: Not available
Engine (displacement/horsepower): 3.0-liter V12/300 horsepower
0–60 miles per hour: Not available
Top speed: 168 miles per hour

was inspired by Ferrari's Grand Prix race cars and featured pontoon-style front fenders that provided better cooling airflow to the brakes. The car's aggressive look was accentuated by its bulging hood, created to provide clearance for the half-dozen Weber carburetors atop its 3.0-liter V12 engine.

One of the cars ran as high as second at Le Mans. The prototypes raced again in the last

race of the season, showing the car's potential with third- and fourth-place finishes.

Taking its name from the red color used on its cylinder heads, the Ferrari 250 Testa Rossa ("red head" in Italian) made its official debut in late November 1957 at Maranello.

The car had a tube-frame chassis, double-wishbone front suspension, DeDion rear axle, and drum brakes (which were upgraded to discs for 1959). The red-headed engine, designed by the legendary Gioachino Colombo, supplied 300 horsepower and could propel the car to speeds approaching 170 miles per hour.

The Ferrari 250 Testa Rossa (TR) made its official racing debut at the start of the 1958 season. Driven by the likes of Phil Hill, Peter Collins, Luigi Musso, and Olivier Gendebien, the new Ferrari won four of six races that

season—Gendebien and Hill winning at Le Mans—and brought Ferrari its third consecutive world sports car championship.

With Scaglietti busy building Ferrari road cars, the TR got new bodywork for 1959, this time styled by Pininfarina. It won at Sebring, but Aston Martin took the season championship.

By 1960, the TR was basically a four-year-old car, yet Gendebien and Paul Frere won at Le Mans and by the end of the season Ferrari had regained the constructors' championship.

By 1961, the car was ancient, yet Gendebien and Hill won at Sebring and Le Mans. Even in 1962, an evolution of the car won yet again at Le Mans.

Did You Know?

Counting the early prototypes and 330 TR1/LM that won Le Mans in 1962, as many as 34 TRs were built. The cars have become among the most highly prized by car collectors, demanding prices in excess of $10 million at auctions or private sales.

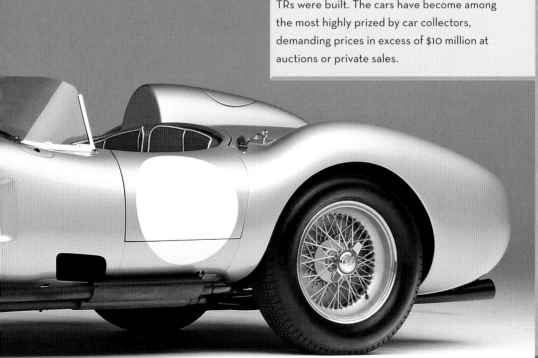

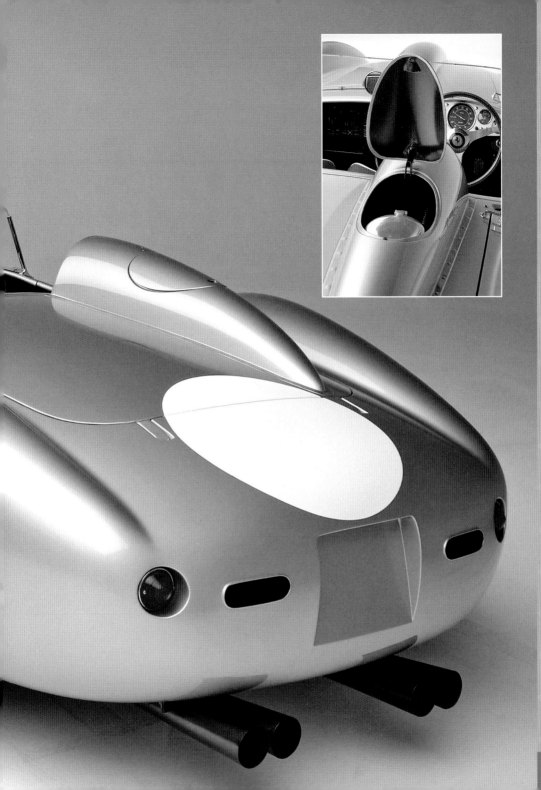

The California Spyder wasn't the first Ferrari convertible, but it has become the most desirable.

Pinin Farina showed the prototype for a Ferrari 250 GT Cabriolet at the Geneva show early in 1957, and 36 of what would become known as the PF Cabriolet were built. The smooth-sided car was elegant and based on a relatively luxurious 250 grand touring coupe also developed by Pinin Farina.

But while the car was gorgeous—Woolworth heiress and actress Barbara Hutton was among the 36 original owners—it lacked an edge. American Ferrari distributor Luigi Chinetti and West Coast dealer John von Neumann had customers who wanted a roadster more like the racy 250 GT Tour de France coupe.

So, just as the PF Cabriolet was going into production, Ferrari had Pinin Farina design another roadster, this one to be tweaked and produced by Scaglietti, which had been building so many successful Ferrari racing cars. Because of its American and especially sunny

West Coast target buyer, the car was called the California Spyder.

The car was both gorgeous and racy. Three were built with aluminum bodies specifically for racing. Richie Ginther and Howard Hively drove one to the GT class victory at Sebring in 1959 and later that year Chinetti's North American Racing Team version was fifth overall at Le Mans, with Bob Grossman and Fernand Tavano alternating behind the steering wheel.

250 GT CALIFORNIA SPYDER

Years produced: 1957–1960
Number produced: 52
Price: $13,600
Engine (displacement/horsepower): 3.0-liter V12/240 horsepower
0–60 miles per hour: 6.5 seconds
Top speed: 145 miles per hour

Did You Know?

A short-wheelbase version of the California Spyder was introduced for 1960. Actor James Coburn bought a 1961 model. Four decades later, the former Coburn California Spyder sold for more than $10.8 million at a classic car auction.

250 GT CALIFORNIA SPYDER

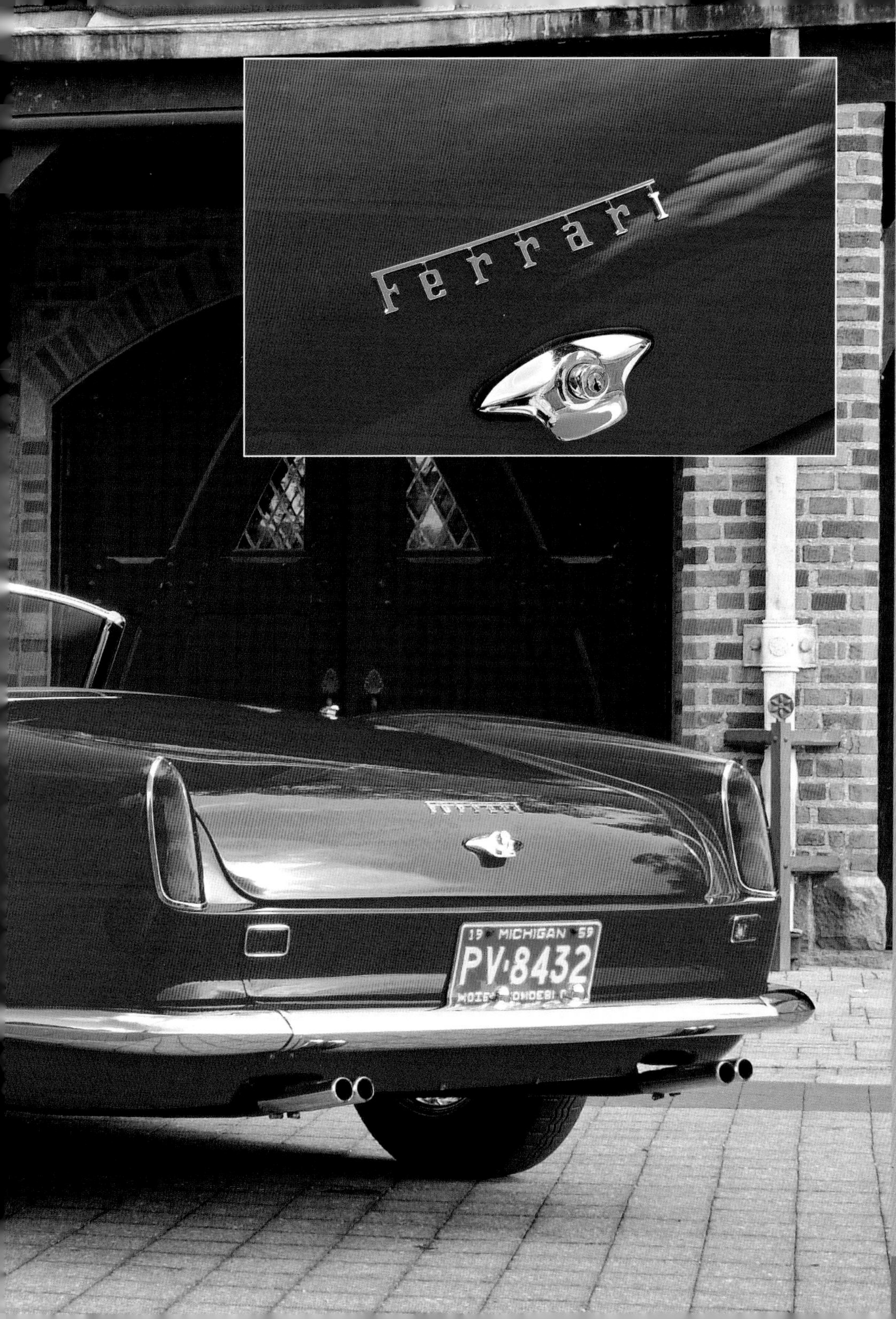
Ferrari
19 MICHIGAN 59
PV·8432

As a popular chef might put it, Ferrari "kicked it up a notch" in 1959 when it introduced a new version of the 250 GT. This new car, introduced at the Paris show, was built on a shortened wheelbase—reduced from nearly 102.4 inches (2,600 millimeters) to less than 94.5 inches (2,400 millimeters). Though officially still the Ferrari 250 GT, these new cars became known as short-wheelbase cars, or SWB.

But a shortening of the wheelbase wasn't the only change for the Berlinetta coupe—built in either competition or "luxury" versions—and

250 GT SWB BERLINETTA

Years produced: 1959–1962
Number produced: 165
Price: $12,500
Engine (displacement/horsepower): 3.0-liter V12/240–300 horsepower
0–60 miles per hour: 6.5 seconds
Top speed: 145 miles per hour

the California Spyder roadster. This new series of 250 GTs was equipped with disc brakes at each corner. Early cars also wore all-aluminum

bodies. Design was by Pinin Farina with metal work by Scaglietti.

Shorter, lighter, more nimble, and quicker stopping, with a 3.0-liter V12 fed by three carburetors and with 9.2:1 compression generating as much as 280 horsepower, the SWB Ferraris were a terror on the track and on the street.

Competing against the likes of the Aston Martin DB4GT, Chevrolet Corvette, and new Jaguar E-type, the SWB Ferrari led all GT category cars at Le Mans in 1960 and 1961, won the Tour de France from 1960 to 1962, and posted victories in the Goodwood Tourist Trophy races in 1960 and 1961 with Stirling Moss at the wheel.

Did You Know?

Nineteen specially prepared 250 GT SWB competition Berlinettas became known as the SEFAC (Scuderia Enzo Ferrari Auto Corse) "Hot Rods." The cars, officially known within Ferrari as the Comp/61 cars, were built on lighter but more rigid frames and had very thin aluminum bodies and engines topped by six carburetors, creating some 300 horsepower.

250 GT SWB BERLINETTA

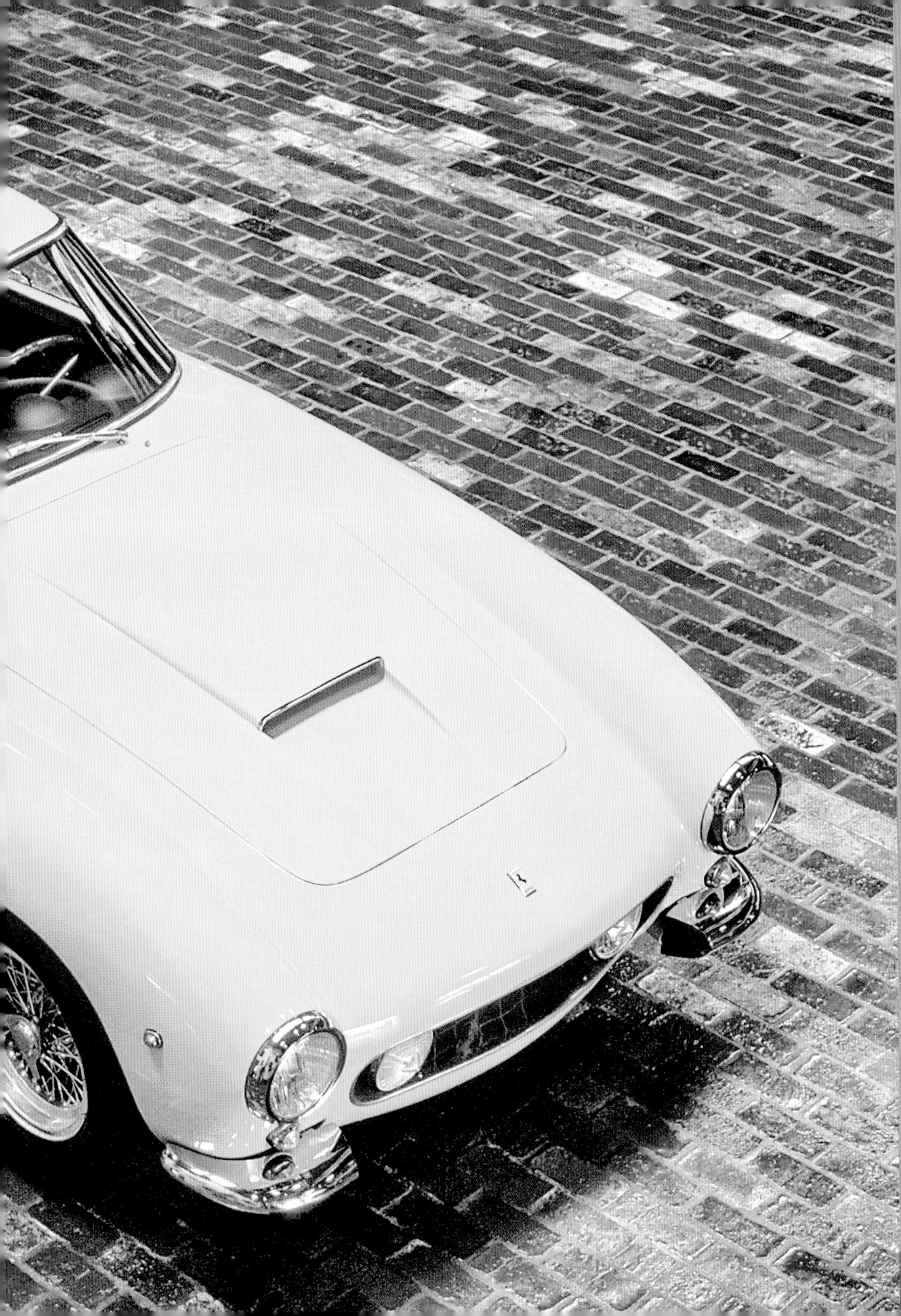

250 GT SWB BERLINETTA

A change in rules for the 1962 sports-car racing season meant the world championship would be determined by success not in prototype categories but in the road car–based grand touring division.

Thus, in late February, when Ferrari held its annual open house, the 250 GTO sat next to Ferrari's latest Grand Prix racer. GTO stands for *Gran Turismo Omologata*, or Grand Touring Homologation. To be homologated for the new racing rules, an automaker needed to manufacture 100 such vehicles, but because of similarities in their chassis and other components, Ferrari was able to convince the powers that be that this purpose-built race car wasn't a separate model. It was merely an evolution of its short-wheelbase competition coupe for road and track.

But instead of a Pininfarina-designed body, this GTO wore sheet metal that was sculpted in the wind tunnel by Ferrari engineer Giotto Bizzarrini. Oh, you might take your GTO out on the road for a grand tour, but if you did, the car's battery and an oil tank crowded your passenger's feet, and instead of space for luggage there was room only for the mandatory spare tire in the tiny trunk.

With its low, long nose, rear deck spoiler, and Ferrari 12-cylinder power, the GTO could exceed 170 miles per hour on the Mulsanne Straight at Le Mans.

The GTO had been under development since early in 1961. Though it wouldn't make an official debut until the 1962 Sebring 12-hour, a GTO prototype was entered in the 3-hour race at Daytona, where Stirling Moss drove it to fourth overall and first in the now even more important GT category. Then, at Sebring, with Phil Hill and Olivier Gendebien at the wheel, the car finished second overall and, again, first in GT.

250 GTO

Years produced: 1961–1964
Number produced: 37
Price: $18,000
Engine (displacement/horsepower): 3.0-liter V12/300 horsepower
0–60 miles per hour: 5 seconds
Top speed: 170 miles per hour

Did You Know?

As they were finishing the GTO and getting ready to start testing, Enzo Ferrari fired several of his leading engineers, including Giotto Bizzarrini and Carlo Chiti, leaving the testing and completion of the championship-winning race car to 25-year-old Mauro Forghieri, who would also create cars that won four World Driving (Grand Prix) championships between 1964 and 1979.

"Perhaps the most pure design ever to be created by Pininfarina." That's what the author of the *Standard Catalog of Ferrari, 1947–2003* calls the Ferrari 250 GT Berlinetta Lusso, or GTL model, unveiled at the Paris show in 1962.

"This car," he continues, "was meant for those who longed for the looks of the legendary GTO but required more civilized road manners."

Those manners not only applied to the car's dynamic capabilities, but to its accoutrements.

250 GT BERLINETTA LUSSO

Years produced: 1962–1964
Number produced: 351
Price: $12,600
Engine (displacement/horsepower): 3.0-liter V12/250 horsepower
0–60 miles per hour: 6.9 seconds
Top speed: 150 miles per hour

Lusso was the Italian word for *luxury*, and the interior was done in fine leather and carpet, with two seats, and behind them two leather straps to secure luggage.

The chassis was similar to the GTO's chassis, though made from steel tubing of smaller diameter and with its V12 engine mounted more forward to provide more room inside for people. The engine was a detuned version of the GTO's, though still pumped out 250 horsepower, and that figure could be boosted by optional heads and carburetors.

The 250 GTL was the last in the line of the Ferrari 250s. Among the car's owners group was actor Steve McQueen, whose "Marrone Metallizzato" (brown color) 1936 GTL sold at a collector car auction for $2.3 million in 2007.

Did You Know?
Battista Pininfarina liked the GTL so much he had a special one built by Scaglietti as his personal daily driver.

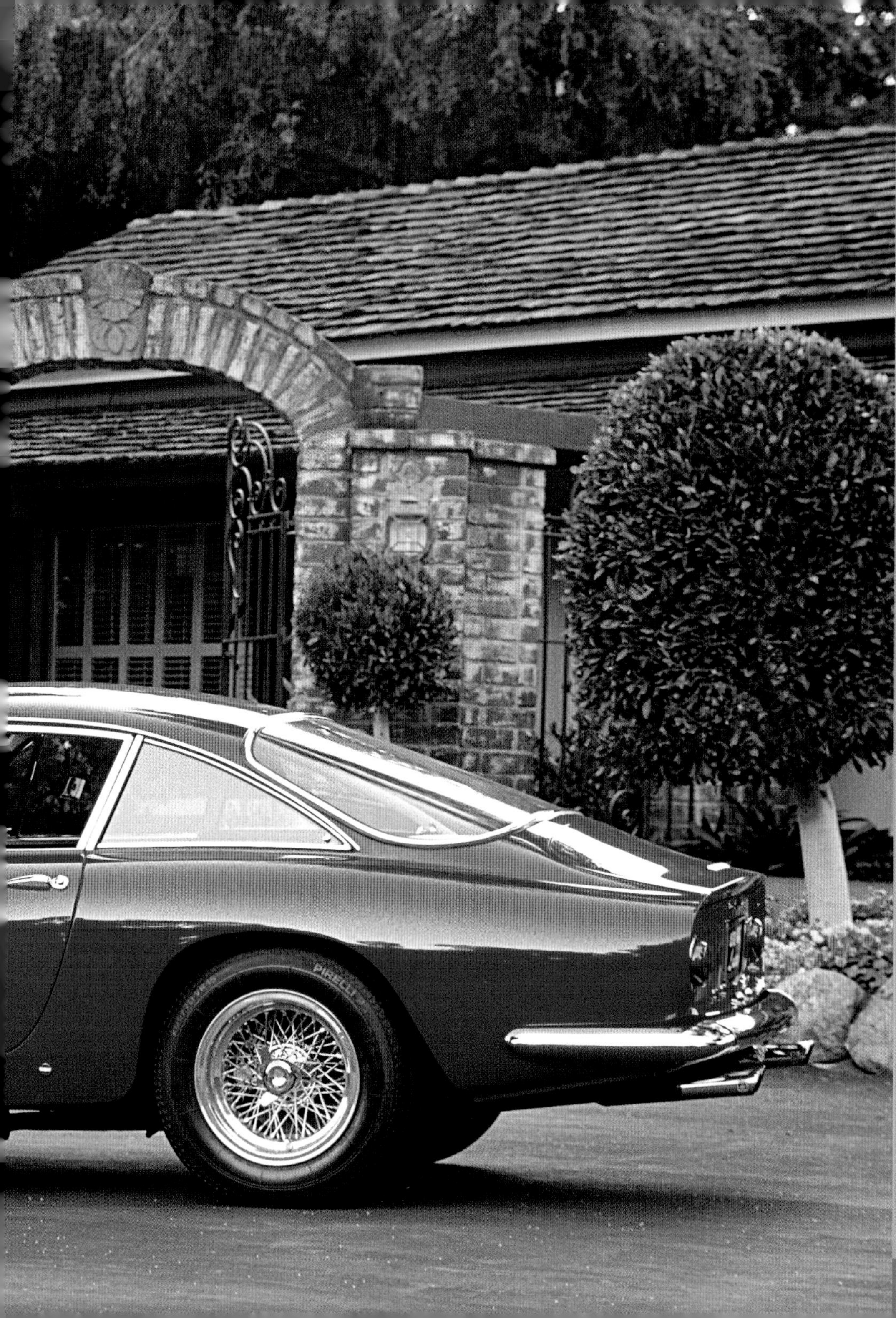

250 GT BERLINETTA LUSSO

Production of Ferrari's 400 Superamerica model ended in 1963, and the company didn't wait long to introduce its new top-of-the-line Grand Touring machine. The 500 Superfast was unveiled early in 1964 at the Geneva show.

The 500 Superfast was built on a chassis based on Ferrari's 330 GT 2+2 and carried a new 5.0-liter V12 engine that created an astounding

FERRARI 500 SUPERFAST

Years produced: 1964–1966
Number produced: 37
Price: $24,400
Engine (displacement/horsepower): 5.0-liter V12/400 horsepower
0–60 miles per hour: Not available
Top speed: 150 miles per hour

400 horsepower. But what made the car impressive was its design—both inside and out.

Outside, the car wore a sleek but elegant Pininfarina coach-built body. Inside, the car features Connolly leather.

The car was produced in two series, I and II, with Series II coming with a five-speed instead of four-speed transmission and with air conditioning and power steering as options.

Among other options was the buyer's choice of front quarter-panel air extractors with the traditional 11 louvers or with three larger vents.

The 500 Superfast was the last of the very limited production Ferraris and was intended,

Ferrari said at the time, for "sovereigns, performers, and great industrialists."

Of the 36 500 Superfasts built (the 37th married a Superfast body with a 330 GT engine), a dozen were exported to the United States and 10 more originally were sold in England.

Did You Know?

The Ferrari 500 Superfast could be equipped with an "assist" that allowed the driver to open the passenger's door without moving out from behind the steering wheel.

FERRARI 500 SUPERFAST

Production of Ferrari's famed 250 models ended in the fall of 1964, just about the time the company was unveiling at the Paris show the successor to that historic line. The new car, the 275, was displayed in GTB coupe and GTS open-topped roadster versions, and instead of merely hacking off the car's roof, the GTS gained its own unique Pininfarina-designed rear bodywork. Whether with closed or open top, the 275 GTB and 275 GTS have come to be cherished among the Italian design house's finest works.

But there was much more to this new model than its lovely lines.

The V12 engine was new. The 275 designation came from the fact that each cylinder displaced not 250, but 275 cubic centimeters. This new 3.3-liter V12 yielded 280 horsepower when tuned for the coupe and 260 in the convertible.

To enhance dynamic balance, the five-speed transmission was moved from just behind the engine into unity with the rear differential.

To make the most of this enhanced balance, the 275 GTB and 275 GTS became the first Ferrari road cars to ride on a fully independent suspension.

A racing version of the car was known as the 275 GTC.

In 1966—again in Paris—the car was updated with six instead of three carburetors and four overhead camshafts. The 275 GTB/4 and 275 GTB/S now benefited from 300 horsepower, and the new bulging hoods needed to cover the additional carburetors.

275 GTB

Years produced: 1964–1968
Number produced: 1,100
Price: $13,900
Engine (displacement/horsepower): 3.3-liter V12/280 horsepower
0–60 miles per hour: 6.0 seconds
Top speed: 155 miles per hour

Did You Know?

In 1967, French racer Jean-Pierre Beltoise did a 46-mile road test for *L'Auto Journal*, in which he drove, in seemingly comfortable and almost leisurely fashion, a Ferrari 275 GTB/4 between Pont d'Orleans and Nemours in under 26 minutes—as he put it, "at an average speed of more than one hundred twenty-one miles per hour, which is remarkable enough without noting that I had to stop for the toll gates."

Unveiled at the Geneva show in the spring of 1966, the 330 GTC proved to be the car that one Ferrari expert would come to believe "offered the best balance between elegant understated styling and state-of-the-art handling and performance of the Enzo-era Ferraris."

Another proclaimed that while the engine was almost too quiet, the car had sure-footed handling characteristics nearly on par with the best of the day's pure-bred racing machines.

At the time of its introduction, the 330 GTC was seen as a blending primarily of two other

330 GTC

Years produced: 1966–1968
Number produced: 600
Price: $17,100
Engine (displacement/horsepower): 3.9-liter V12/300 horsepower
0–60 miles per hour: 7.0 seconds
Top speed: 150 miles per hour

Ferrari models—the 275 GTB and the 330 GT, though the design added cues from other cars in the stable, including a grille inspired by the one on the 500 Superfast.

The 330 GTC, and the roadster version—the 330 GTS that was introduced a few months later in the year at Paris—were built on the short-wheelbase version of the 275 GTB, but with the engine and the styling cues from the 330 GT.

The engine was a 3.9-liter V12 that achieved 300 horsepower, though now it was in a car with room for only two instead of four occupants.

Those occupants enjoyed Pininfarina's latest interior design work and a view out a greenhouse that features very thin pillars. Power windows were standard equipment, as was teakwood trim.

Did You Know?

Ferrari has been successful in seemingly every type of racing it has entered, with one exception: Indianapolis. In 1952, Ferrari lengthened and strengthened its Formula One car to produce the Ferrari 375 Indy. Four such cars were entered for qualifying trails for the Indianapolis 500. Only one of them, driven by former world champion Alberto Ascari, qualified—for the 9th of 11 rows. The car made only 41 laps before it was sidelined by a broken hub.

Luigi Chinetti, race-car driver, Ferrari distributor for the United States, and creator of the famed North American Racing Team (NART), convinced Ferrari that it needed to produce a roadster version of its 275 GTB sports coupe. Chinetti saw the car not only as a top-down flagship, but as a car that would be competitive in GT-class motorsports.

The GTS/4 was announced early in 1966, but orders were slow in coming. In fact, only 10 such cars were built—and only one of them was destined for much track time.

GTS/4 NART SPYDER

Year produced: 1967
Number produced: 10
Price: Not available
Engine (displacement/horsepower): 3.3-liter V12/300 horsepower
0-60 miles per hour: Not available
Top speed: 155 miles per hou

To try to hype the car, Chinetti entered one in the 1967 12-hour race at Sebring, and recruited an all-woman driving team—Denis

McCluggage and Marianne "Pinkie" Rollo. Instead of the full NART effort, the basically stock car was entered under the NVRT (Northern Vermont Racing Team) banner. Lo and behold: The car was the highest-finished Ferrari in the race, taking 17th overall and 2nd in the GTS category.

That same car was repainted and was driven by Steve McQueen in the movie *The Thomas Crown Affair*. McQueen also bought one of the other nine GTS/4 NART Spyders.

The GTS/4 featured an enhanced drivetrain that made it capable of speeds of more than 150 miles per hour.

Did You Know?

Born in Italy, Luigi Chinetti came to the United States in 1940 for the Indianapolis 500 and stayed through the war. He became a U.S. citizen in 1946. He was the first three-time winning driver in the 24 Hours of Le Mans (in 1932 and 1934 with Alfa Romeo and in 1949 with Ferrari). He drove in every Le Mans event between 1932 and 1953.

CHAPTER 3
THE ROADSHOW SH
INTO OVERDRIVE

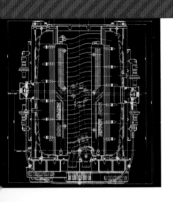

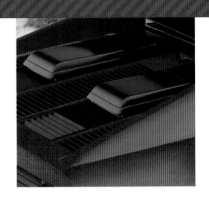

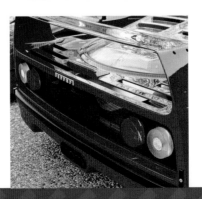

FTS

Enzo Ferrari's passion was auto racing. But to finance his racing teams, he had to continue developing new cars for wealthy customers to drive on public roads. Weary of such financial realities, and with world economics affecting his customer base, Ferrari used intermediaries to approach Henry Ford II about a deal that would put the Ferrari road car brand under Ford's control while allowing Ferrari to continue focusing his passion on auto racing. Just as the deal was to be consummated, Ferrari changed his mind—or perhaps it was a change of heart. Instead, he sold a portion of his company—and before long, half-interest—to Italian automaker Fiat.

Ford's response was to launch a motorsports effort that would achieve revenge by beating Ferrari—first at Le Mans and later with Ford-powered Grand Prix racers. But Ferrari would rally, winning Formula One championships in the mid-1970s and, with financial and technical help from its Italian benefactor, by producing a succession of nothing short of sensational road cars.

Those cars would include such icons as the Testarossa, with its straked sides and wedge shape, the high-winged F40 and F50, and even a gorgeous sports car named for Ferrari's deceased son.

Enzo Ferrari's son, Alfredino, was an engineer and champion of the development of a V-6 engine that eventually carried Mike Hawthorn to the 1958 Grand Prix racing championship.

But "Dino," as he was called, didn't get to celebrate that championship. He died two years earlier from a kidney disease.

As early as 1965, at Paris, Pininfarina and Ferrari began showing a succession of "Dino" V-6–powered concept cars.

Finally, in 1967, the Dino 206 GT went into production and was historic on more than one count. First, the car was Ferrari's first mid-engine sports car for the street. Second, the car

DINO 206 GT

Years produced: 1967–1974
Number produced: 150 206 GT; 2,500 246 GT and GTS
Price: $13,400
Engine (displacement/horsepower): 2.0-liter V-6/180 horsepower
0–60 miles per hour: 7.1 seconds
Top speed: 145 miles per hour

wore no Ferrari badge. Instead of the prancing horse on a shield-shaped emblem, the car had a rectangular yellow emblem with "Dino" written in script.

Ferrari's goal was that the car would give his company a volume competitor for vehicles such as Porsche and other small-displacement sports cars, and 500 copies would be needed for the car to be eligible for racing. To produce that many, Ferrari had Fiat manufacture the engine. Fiat used its own engines, but put those engines in front of the driver not behind, as in the

Ferrari version. Also, while Ferrari's Dino V-6s were tuned to 180 horsepower, Fiat's produced only 160.

Soon, the engine's displacement grew to 2.4 liters, thus the Dino 246 GT from 1969.

Did You Know?
The Dino V-6 engine developed by Alfredino Ferrari and Vittorio Jano was used in both Formula and sports racers before going into the Dino sports car. In 1973, the engine, now tuned to put forth 300 horsepower, was used to power the Lancia Stratos, which it propelled to three World Rally Championships.

When Ferrari unveiled the 275 GTB/4 at the Paris show in 1967, the reaction was, well, disappointment. Lamborghini had just introduced the first modern supercar—the sleek mid-engined Miura—and Ferrari's response was really nothing more than a carryover model, albeit the first Ferrari road car with a V12 equipped with double overhead camshafts.

Among the disappointed was a young designer, Leonardo Fioravanti, whose first work at Pininfarina had been the design of the

365 GTB/4 DAYTONA

Years produced: 1968–1974
Number produced: 1,400
Price: $2,650
Engine (displacement/horsepower): 4.4-liter V12/352 horsepower
0–60 miles per hour: 5.9 seconds
Top speed: 175 miles per hour

Dino 206 GT. Within a week of long nights, Fioravanti had redesigned Ferrari's new car, and while he couldn't change the front-engine

architecture, he did push the envelope on Pininfarina's "Superfast" design language.

The result, unveiled at Paris in 1968, was the 365 GTB/4, nicknamed and forever known as the Daytona in honor of Ferrari's 1-2-3 sweep over Porsche and Ford in the 24 Hours of Daytona race.

Nobody seemed disappointed in this car, which drew praises that ranged all the way up to being called "a poem in steel."

Propelling this poem from a standing start to 60 miles per hour in under six seconds and on to a top speed of 175 miles per hour was a 4.4-liter V12 that breathed through six carburetors and produced 352 horsepower.

And with the engine set well back in the chassis, the car had amazing balance. Add in an aerodynamic body, and the Daytona was even faster than Lamborghini's so-called supercar.

Did You Know?

Why was the Daytona officially known as the 365 GTB/4? The number 365 represented the displacement of each of the engine's 12 cylinders, in cubic centimeters. GTB stood for *Gran Turisimo Berlinetta*. The /4 signified the engine's four-cam architecture.

The 1975 Paris Motor Show provided the scene for the unveiling of a car that would be produced in volumes that would surpass all Ferraris built in the first two decades of the company's history. This car was the Ferrari 308 GTB, the V-8–powered replacement for the V-6–propelled Dino 246.

Like the Dino, the 308 GTB (Gran Turismo Berlinetta) had its engine mounted midship, just behind its pair of seats.

The body in which the driver, passenger, and V-8 engine rode was designed by Pininfarina and built by Scaglietti. It established a design

308

Years produced: 1975–1984
Number produced: 21,678
Price: 308 GTB: $28,500
308 GTBi: $40,576
308 GTB Qv: $55,145
308 GTS Qv: $60,345
Engine (displacement/horsepower): 2.9-liter V-8/240 horsepower (later reduced to meet new emission standards, then increased to 230 horsepower with four-valve heads)
0–60 miles per hour: 7–8 seconds
Top speed: 155 miles per hour

language that would mark Ferraris for the next couple of decades. That design featured hidden headlamps incorporated into a wedge-like nose over a wide, egg-crate grille, cove-style air intakes that started in the door panels and extended back to just ahead of the rear wheel wells, and a flying-buttress roof that led to an abrupt, Kamm-type tail that featured a quartet of large, round taillamps.

Ferrari used the 1977 Geneva Motor Show to roll out the 308 GTS with a Targa-style roof so the section over the occupants' heads could be removed for open-air driving.

Instead of rear quarter windows, the GTS has louvered panels.

In 1980, Ferrari replaced the quartet of carburetors with fuel injection, thus the 308 GTBi and GTSi.

Two years later, the V-8 engine got four-valve "Quattrovalvole" cylinder heads, thus the 308 GTB Qv model.

Did You Know?

The 308 is probably the most widely recognized of all Ferraris, thanks to the *Magnum, P.I.* television series, that featured Hawaii-based private investigator Thomas Magnum (actor Tom Selleck) driving a bright red 308 GTB.

308

It was at the Turin Motor Show in 1971 that Ferrari finally displayed a grand touring sports coupe with a V12 engine mounted behind the driver. That car went into production in 1973 as the 365 GT/4 BB, the BB short for Berlinetta Boxer. The name *Boxer* indicated the presence of a so-called flat V12, an engine with its pistons horizontally opposed on either side of the crankshaft, pumping back and forth much like a boxer's jab.

512 BERLINETTA BOXER

Years produced: 1976–1984
Number produced: 2,300
Price: $85,000
Engine (displacement/horsepower): 5.0-liter flat 12/360 horsepower
0–60 miles per hour: 7.2 seconds
Top speed: 185 miles per hour

In 1976, the 365 GT/4 BB evolved into the 512 BB. The car itself was little changed. There was a slight front lip spoiler, two fewer taillamps, and the addition of NACA-style air intakes just ahead of the rear wheels, and a repositioned fuel filler.

The engine was enlarged from the former 4.4-liters to 5.0, however, and a change in nomenclature turned 365 (cubic centimeters of displacement per cylinder) into 512 (5 liters, 12 cylinders). Horsepower increased from 344 to 360, and torque grew from barely more than 300 to 333 lb-ft.

In 1981, the engine's quartet of carburetors was replaced by fuel injectors. Horsepower dropped (to 340), but so did emissions. A dividend was that overall drivability of the car also improved, with power flowing smoothly throughout the rev range.

Did You Know?

Karl Benz patented the design of a "boxer" engine with horizontally opposed pistons in 1896. Volkswagen, Porsche, and Subaru have made extensive use of boxer-engine architecture.

For 1976, Ferrari introduced a somewhat shocking new range-topping grand-touring model—the Ferrari 400 GT. The car was shocking not because of its design—it was largely based on the previous 365 GT/4—but because it carried a three-speed Turbo Hydra-Matic automatic transmission built by General Motors. This marked the first time Ferrari offered a car without a clutch pedal and manually shifted gearbox. A three-speed

400I GT

Years produced: 1976–1985
Number produced: 1,700
Price: Not available
Engine (displacement/horsepower): 4.9-liter V12/320–340 horsepower
0–60 miles per hour: Not available
Top speed: Not available

manual was available in the 400 but only as optional equipment.

At launch, the 4.9-liter V12 engine was fed by half a dozen carburetors, but in 1979 that setup was replaced by fuel injection, thus the 400i model. The change from carburetors to injection bumped horsepower from 320 to 340.

Though based on the 365 GT/4, the 400 and 400i GTs featured a new front lip spoiler, new taillamps, and lug nuts instead of knockoff hubs to secure its wheels. Inside, the front seats automatically slid forward when the seat backs were tipped, thus allowing easier access to the back seats. Also new was a four-speaker stereo system with a tape deck.

The car wasn't certified by Ferrari for U.S. sales, but several came anyway through the so-called gray market.

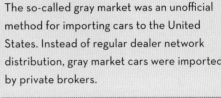

Did You Know?

The so-called gray market was an unofficial method for importing cars to the United States. Instead of regular dealer network distribution, gray market cars were imported by private brokers.

288 GTO

Ferrari resurrected two historic names for the 1984 model year—Testarossa and GTO.

Though the 288 GTO may have looked like the Ferrari 308/328 coupe, its wheelbase had been stretched 4 inches so its mid-mounted engine could be positioned longitudinally rather than transversely. That V-8 engine displaced only 2.9 liters, but it had two turbochargers and four camshafts and pulled off 400 horsepower through a five-speed manual gearbox.

To keep such power under control, the 288 GTO rode on wide tires beneath blistered

288 GTO

Years produced: 1984–1985
Number produced: 272
Price: $83,400
Engine (displacement/horsepower): Twin-turbocharged 2.9-liter V-8/400 horsepower
0–60 miles per hour: 5.0 seconds
Top speed: 189 miles per hour

fenders and featured air spoilers both front and rear. The car also had four driving lights integrated into its grille.

The 288 GTO was designed to meet international Group B racing regulations. Though the category didn't succeed, Ferrari went ahead with production of its new supercar, which featured such materials as Kevlar and Nomex composite, aluminum, fiberglass, and carbon fiber in its internal construction.

The interior was racy as well, with a suede-covered dashboard, Veglia gauges, Momo steering wheel, and cloth seats. Features such as leather seats, air conditioning, power windows, and a cassette audio system were available as options.

The new GTO was shown at Geneva early in 1984. Demand from Ferrari faithful was so strong that the company increased its intended 200-vehicle production run.

Did You Know?

The 400-horsepower, 2.9-liter V-8 that powered the 288 GTO was originally developed for use in Lancias competing in the World Rally Championship. Like Ferrari, Lancia was one of the marques operating beneath the Fiat umbrella.

288 GTO

154

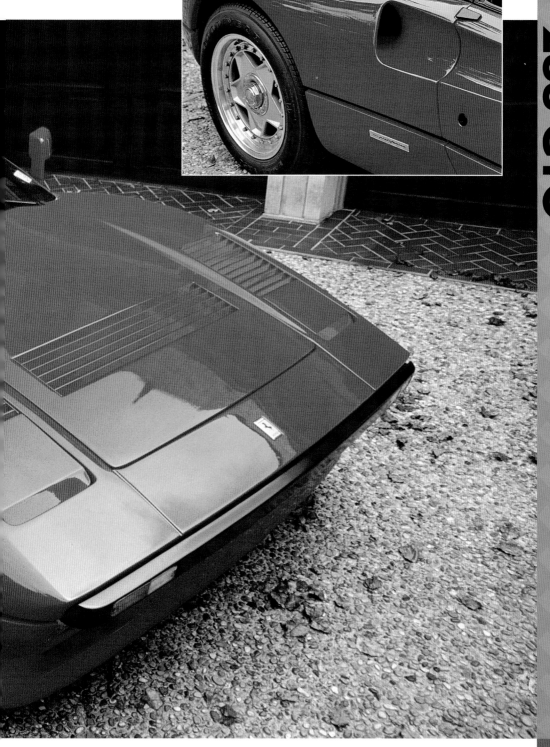

288 GTO

Issues with Ferrari's 512 BB (Berlinetta Boxer) were heat in the interior and a lack of space for luggage. Wow, did Ferrari and Pininfarina find an interesting way to overcome those issues when it came to designing a successor.

That successor was the Ferrari Testarossa, a car with one of the most dramatic looks in the history of the automobile.

Unveiled at the Paris show—well, actually at the famed and glitzy Lido nightclub—the Testarossa (now one word) was a wide wedge

TESTAROSSA 512M

Years produced: 1984–1990
Number produced: nearly 7,200
Price: $90,170
Engine (displacement/horsepower): 5.0-liter 12-cylinder/390 horsepower
0–60 miles per hour: 5.3 seconds
Top speed: 180 miles per hour

of a machine marked by a series of "strakes" (some called them cheese graters, some said egg

slicers) that started just behind the front wheel wells and ran back into the oh-so-wide rear fenders needed to enclose rear wheels that were a startling 10 inches wide.

But those strakes served not only an aesthetic purpose but a practical one. They fed air into a pair of rear-mounted radiators. By putting the radiators behind instead of in front of the driver and occupant, it left room up front for a small trunk, and for cooling air to reach the cockpit, which also benefited from standard air conditioning, as well as hand-sown, leather-covered power seats.

With a 5.0-liter, horizontally opposed 12-cylinder engine attaining 390 horsepower, this low-slung, aerodynamic car was fast and a blast to drive, though not so much to park, what with all that width and not a lot of rearward visibility.

Not to worry: Valets were quite happy to put such an attention-grabber right up front.

Did You Know?

In 1989, the Testarossa was succeeded by the 512M, which offered 428 horsepower from its flat 12, and then, in 1994, the third iteration was introduced in the form of the 440-horsepower F512 M. The F512 M was the last Ferrari with a rear-mounted 12-cylinder engine until the Enzo came along.

The Ferrari F40 was significant not just because it was designed to celebrate the 40th anniversary of Ferrari as an automobile manufacturer, but because it was the last car that Enzo Ferrari personally unveiled.

Ferrari showed the car to the world on July 21, 1987. The following summer, at the age of 90, *il Commendatore* was dead, but his legend lived on in cars such as the F40.

The F40 wasn't merely the fastest Ferrari production car ever built; it was the fastest street-legal car in the world, capable of speeds in excess of 200 miles per hour. It also was the

F40

Year produced: 1988
Number produced: more than 1,300
Price: $399,150
Engine (displacement/horsepower): twin-turbo-charged 3.0-liter V-8/478 horsepower
0–60 miles per hour: 3.9 seconds
Top speed: 201 miles per hour

most expensive car in the world, with a base price of $399,150.

Though its appearance was almost beyond belief with its tall rear wing, the F40 was the

successor—at least spiritually—to the 280 GTO. And like the *Gran Turismo Omologato*, the F40 was created as much for the racetrack as for the road.

But while built over a chassis similar to the 308 GTB, the F40's was stretched to make room for a latitudinally placed and twin-turbocharged engine and five-speed manual transmission. The powertrain produced 478 horsepower, and for those who wanted even more, there were optional turbos and cams that provided another 200 horses.

Though longer and wider than the GTO, the use of carbon fiber and Kevlar; of a clear plastic engine cover; and the elimination of such things as carpeting, radio, and power windows made the F40 more than 100 pounds lighter: Zero-to-60 in under four seconds, a buck and a quarter in 12 seconds, and a top speed of 201 miles per hour.

Did You Know?

Though the F40 came without carpeting, radio, and power windows, air conditioning was an option. The car also came with a driver's seat custom-fitted to its new owner.

F4O

Ferrari introduced its new four-seat grand touring coupe at Paris in 1992. The 456 GT was stunning, and not just because it was unveiled wearing beautiful metallic blue paint. That metallic blue hue was affixed to an elegant and sculptural body designed by Pininfarina.

The body side featured a large, forward-leaning scallop that ran from behind the front wheelwells through the doors and into the rear quarter panels. Although the hood had to cover a 5.5-liter V12, the profile was low with the greenhouse arcing smoothly back into a short rear deck that had the hint of a spoiler.

Though elegant, and with a luxurious interior that could seat four people in 2+2 style, the 456 GT looked fast. And it was—so fast that a rear spoiler deployed from beneath the rear bumper

at speeds of more than 75 miles per hour to enhance high-speed stability.

The car could achieve high speeds. The 442-horsepower engine could be linked to a five-speed manual or four-speed automatic transmission, the latter known as the 456 GTA. In combination with the aerodynamic shape, the powertrain provided a top speed approaching 190 miles per hour.

456 GT

Years produced: 1992–1997
Number produced: 1,900
Price: $224,800
Engine (displacement/horsepower): 5.5-liter V12/442 horsepower
0–60 miles per hour: 5.1 seconds
Top speed: Nearly 190 miles per hour

Did You Know?

The first Formula One/World Driving Championship race—the Grand Prix of Europe—was held in May 1950 at the Silverstone circuit in England. Ferrari's entry was the 275 F1, powered by a 3.3-liter V12 and driven by Alberto Ascari. Ferrari has been racing in F1 ever since.

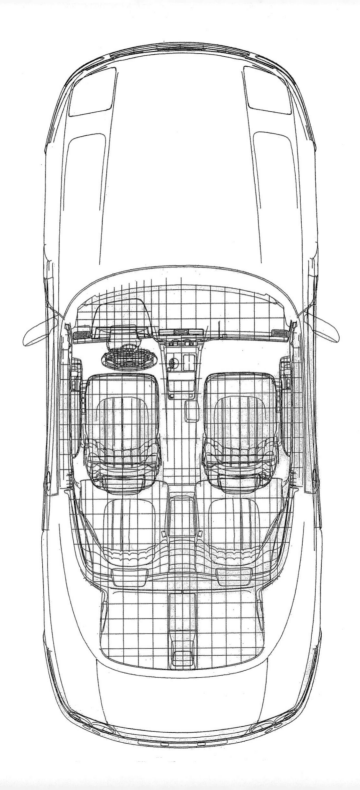

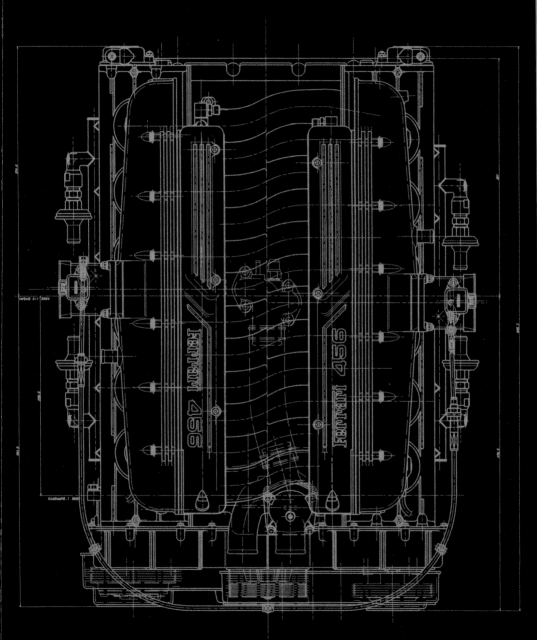

The replacement for Ferrari's popular 308/328 line was less than warmly received. The new 348 TB and TS were launched at the 1989 Frankfurt show in 1989. Some thought the use of Testarossa-style side strakes detracted from the design. Some found the car's road manners less than polite. Some noted that the new Acura NSX provided better performance at little more than half the price.

Ferrari responded by producing what were known as 348 Series Speciales, at first enhanced variations of both the TB coupe and the Targa-roofed TS Spyder.

348 SERIES SPECIALE

Years produced: 1993–1995
Number produced: 1,450
Price: $131,000
Engine (displacement/horsepower): 3.4-liter V-8/312 horsepower
0–60 miles per hour: 5.6 seconds
Top speed: 175 miles per hour

The Speciale models received revised suspension, widened rear track, less restrictive exhaust systems (increasing the output of the 3.4-liter V-8 engine to 312 horsepower), new front spoiler and modified taillamps, F-40–style seats, and monochrome paint instead of blacked-out lower body sides.

Ferrari also created a special racing version of the car and launched the 348 Challenge racing series. Each North American Ferrari dealership was required to support at least one customer entrant in a regional competition that would send its champion to a world finals in Italy.

Then, for the 1992 model year, Ferrari added one more 348 Series Speciale to the lineup—a true convertible—the Spider—the first two-seat Ferrari convertible since the Daytona Spyder of the 1970s.

Did You Know?
The *T* in the names of the 348 TB and TS came from the transverse placement of the transmission in relation to the 3.4-liter V-8 engine.

Ferrari used the annual late summer classic car and vintage racing celebration on California's Monterey Peninsula to unveil its newest V-8 model—the F355, which was available at first as a coupe or Targa-topped spyder. A year later, a true convertible—the first from Ferrari with a power top—joined the lineup. Finally came the F355 F1 with Grand Prix racing–style, steering wheel–mounted gear-shift paddles to control its six-speed gearbox.

But even before the Formula One–style shifter, there were direct ties between the

F355

Years produced: 1994–1999
Number produced: 11,300
Price: $130,000
Engine (displacement/horsepower): 3.5-liter V-8/375 horsepower
0–60 miles per hour: 4.7 seconds
Top speed: 183 miles per hour

racetrack and the roadway in the F355, which had a racing-style flat bottom to enhance high-speed grip. The car's body, which featured a

pair of air scoops along the trailing edge of each door and a flying buttress rear roofline, also was sculpted in the wind tunnel.

Suspension for the F355 was active, with onboard electronics adjusting to road, speed, and steering inputs.

And, as with previous V-8s, there was a special racing version for the 355 Challenge series, with brakes from the F40, a carbon-fiber front fascia with large ducts to cool those brakes, as well as a revised suspension and an oil cooler.

Did You Know?

Ferrari again changed engine nomenclature when it introduced the F355. The number 355 didn't represent individual cylinder displacement or the number of cylinders, but represented the V-8 engine's 3,500cc capacity and its five-valves-per-cylinder heads.

To celebrate his company's 40th anniversary, and to make sure his legacy included at least one more supercar, Enzo Ferrari commissioned Pininfarina to design the F40, an ultra-exotic and high-winged road car that looked like it belonged on the racetrack. The F40 would, indeed, become part of Ferrari's legacy; it also would be the last car *il Commendatore* would personally unveil. The F40 made its debut on July 21, 1987. A year later, Ferrari died at the age of 90.

To commemorate the 50th anniversary of Ferrari, albeit a few years early, and to provide a worthy successor to the F40, the aptly named F50 was introduced at the Geneva Motor Show in the spring of 1995.

In many respects, the design proposal for the F50 was quite simple: build what was basically a Ferrari Formula One racing car that could be driven on public roads.

While Grand Prix racers of the era were limited to engines of 3.5 liters in displacement, there were no such restrictions on supercars such as the F50. Thus the F50 carried a mid-rear mounted 4.7-liter V12 based on the F1 engine. That enlarged engine provided the F50 with 520 horsepower, made available to the rear wheels via a six-speed manual gearbox.

When the car was introduced, Ferrari President Luca di Montezemolo said that while 50 years of Ferrari racing know-how had gone into the development of the road car, it would be the last time Ferrari would be able to base such a car on its Formula One engine. He explained why: much more stringent emission standards were being legislated in all major automotive markets around the world.

Combined with the car's slick aerodynamics and light weight, the powertrain could propel the F50 to speeds in excess of 200 miles per hour.

Ferrari presented the F50 as a Formula One racer "dressed" as a passenger car for public roads.

Though the F50 had a larger engine than did the Ferrari F1 racer, drivers such as Gerhard Berger and Jean Alesi benefited from an engine that revved to more than 17,000 rpm and produced nearly 800 horsepower (Michael Schumacher joined the Ferrari F1 team for 1996).

In many ways, however, the F50 was a racer in road guise. The F50 was comprised primarily of carbon fiber, and while it had fenders over its tires and two seats instead of one, it also had F1-style suspension, underbody panels, and a huge rear wing that created down force, a racing fuel cell–style gasoline tank, and, thanks to a removable roof panel, an open cockpit.

F50

Years produced: 1995–1997
Number produced: 349
Price: $480,000
Engine (displacement/horsepower): 4.7-liter V12/520 horsepower
0–60 miles per hour: 3.7 seconds
Top speed: 202 miles per hour

Did You Know?

Before the start of production, Ferrari's research indicated that the market for such a car would include only 350 buyers. Therefore, only 349 F50 models were built. Why? Because, a Ferrari spokesman explained, Ferraris should be hard to find, and therefore the decision was made to build one car fewer than the market capacity, thus ensuring the car would be have an eager audience.

CHAPTER 4
SUPERCARS FOR A MODERN AGE

Enzo Ferrari died in 1988. He had lived for 90 years. But his legacy lived on in the sinuous shapes of the cars that bore his mark—the Prancing Horse.

When Ferrari died, his Grand Prix drivers hadn't won a championship since the 1979 season. But the team would regroup, adding key technical and managerial personal and a driver named Michael Schumacher, who would win that championship an unprecedented five seasons in a row (2000–2004).

Things didn't slow down at the Ferrari factory, either. Indeed, there was an all-new and ultra-modern car-building facility, and the cars it designed, developed, and produced were equipped with the latest in automotive technology, much of it developed and proven in the heated environment of that ultimate proving ground—Formula One racing.

As a result, Ferrari was selling cars, and in record numbers. In 2002, the company launched a car that not only bore Enzo Ferrari's last name, but his first as well. Like Enzo Ferrari himself, Enzo Ferrari the car represented the pinnacle of automotive enthusiasm and a driving—a driven—passion to excel.

Today, just as in the 1950s and 1960s and the decades since, one word more than any other excites the automotive enthusiast. That word is a name. The name: Ferrari.

Only a very special vehicle would wear the name of the company's hometown, Maranello, and the 550 Maranello was just that—very special.

Introduced in 1996, the 550 Maranello was Ferrari's replacement for the famed and beloved 365 GTB/4 Daytona, one of the most revered vehicles in the company's history, and a vehicle whose production had ended some 22 years earlier, in 1974.

Like the Daytona, the 550 Maranello was a two-seat coupe with a powerful V12 mounted up front, a grand tourer with supercar capability.

550 MARANELLO

Years produced: 1996–2002
Number produced: 3,600
Price: $204,000
Engine (displacement/horsepower): 5.5-liter V12/485 horsepower
0–60 miles per hour: 4.2 seconds
Top speed: 183 miles per hour

In the 550 Maranello, that engine was a 5.5-liter that provided 485 horsepower, thrusting the car from a standing start to 60 miles per hour in barely more than four seconds

and on to a top speed in excess of 180 miles per hour.

The car also featured the latest technology, and a design that used cues from several classic Ferrari models while appearing totally contemporary and modern. As with the Daytona, the nose was long—necessary to cover the V12 powerplant—and the rear deck was short. And while muscular, the car was graceful in its lines and rich in its interior accoutrements.

A 550 Barchetta Pininfarina roadster joined the lineup in 2000.

Did You Know?

Opera's loss was racing's gain. As a child, Ferrari's father took Enzo to auto races and the opera. The young Ferrari expressed a desire to become an opera singer, but he didn't have the voice. As a teenager, Ferrari worked for a local newspaper and wrote several articles about sports, including auto racing.

550 MARANELLO

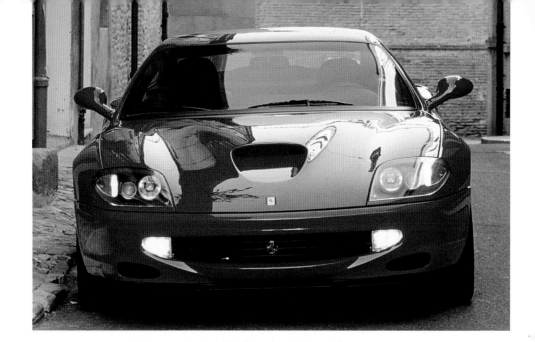

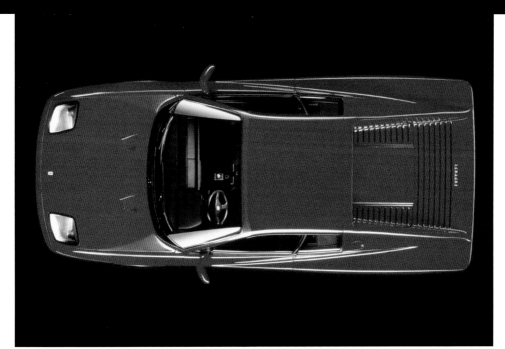

Ford versus Ferrari is a recurring theme. In the late 1960s, it resulted in some historic races at Le Mans; a few decades later, it reignited as Ford began development on its modern supercar, the Ford GT. And the bogey for that exotic, mid-engined and supercharged Ford supercar was the Ferrari 360 Modena.

Introduced at the Geneva show early in 1999, the 360 Modena (the Spyder version would follow a year later), launched the next generation of V-8-powered Ferraris, following in the tire tracks of the 308, 328, 348, and F355.

But the 360 Modena, employing weight-saving engineering and aerodynamic design, was a giant step forward for a truly modern sports car.

The car was built around an aluminum monocoque chassis and tubular steel frame. Suspension was aluminum, as was the body, except for steel roof and door panels.

The five-valve, dry-sump, mid-mounted aluminum engine displaced nearly 3.6-liters and with 11.1:1 compression produced 400 horsepower through a six-speed gearbox that

could be shifted manually or via Formula One–style sequential system. Top speed reached the magic 300 kilometers per hour (186 miles per hour) standard for admission into supercar status.

And yet the 360 Modena wasn't all wings and things. Its carefully engineered underbody helped glue it to the road, allowing its exterior design to be almost elegant, and marked by a change for Ferrari from an open front grille to a more aero-inspired closed nose bracketed by a pair of large outboard air intakes.

360 MODENA AND SPYDER

Years produced: 1999–2005
Number produced: Not available
Price: $138,225
Engine (displacement/horsepower): 3.6-liter V-8/400 horsepower
0–60 miles per hour: 4 seconds
Top speed: 186 miles per hour

Did You Know?

It was a young Sergio Pininfarina who arranged the meeting over lunch in 1951 where his father, Battista "Pinin" and Enzo Ferrari were introduced and first discussed doing business together.

ENZO

There was the Dino, named for Enzo Ferrari's late son, and then, a decade after his own death, Enzo Ferrari's name would be put on a car—the Ferrari Enzo.

What sort of car might be worthy of bearing *il Commendatore*'s name?

Obviously, this had to be the ultimate sports car, capable of high-speed travel on public roads or closed racing circuits. Significantly, the driver who did much of the development work on this new car was multi-time Ferrari world-racing champion Michael Schumacher. The entire Ferrari Formula One racing team got involved in the project, as did several major Ferrari suppliers, and the result was a car that was part sports car/part Formula One racer, and had the appearance of a road-going stealth jet fighter.

The Enzo was unveiled—in Fly Yellow colors—at the Paris Motor Show in 2002, and

it was announced that only 399 copies would be produced, either in the bright yellow hue, in Ferrari red, or in a Stealth-style black.

The price? Oh, $670,000, but that included a flight to the factory in Italy to have the driver's seat and the car's pedals fitted specially to the owner's dimensions.

Propulsion for this ultimate Ferrari came from a 6.0-liter V12 engine that beget 660 horsepower.

ENZO

Years produced: 2002–2003
Number produced: 399
Price: $670,000
Engine (displacement/horsepower): 6.0-liter V12/660 horsepower
0–60 miles per hour: 3.5 seconds
Top speed: 217 miles per hour

Did You Know?

How fast was the Enzo when driven by an expert? Michael Schumacher could lap Ferrari's Fiorano test track in the Enzo five seconds faster than he could in the famed Ferrari F50. Of course, his time on the same track in the Ferrari F1 race car was 30 seconds faster than the Enzo.

ENZO

In 2002 Ferrari replaced the 550 Maranello with the new 575M Maranello. While the sleek coupe may have looked much like its predecessor, it was changed so much beneath its skin that it warranted the M—for modified—designation.

Those modifications included a larger and more powerful engine, using the transmission from Ferrari's Formula One race cars. This was the first such application of this lightning-fast gear-shift technology to a Ferrari with a V12 engine. And where the 550 drew from a 5.5-liter V12 that provided 485 horsepower,

575M MARANELLO
Years produced: 2002–2006
Number produced: Not available
Price: $231,000
Engine (displacement/horsepower): 5.8-liter V12/515 horsepower
0–60 miles per hour: 4.0 seconds
Top speed: 201 miles per hour

the 575 benefited from a 5.8-liter V12 that churned out 515 horsepower. The car also rode on a suspension that automatically adjusted, a technology developed for the Ferrari Enzo.

Inside, the two-seat car was an all-new design with primary gauges clustered into a single housing and seats that adjusted electronically for driver and passenger comfort and proper positioning.

To deal with higher speeds and dynamic capabilities, the bodywork also was modified, especially at the front with a smaller grille. Interior design was new as well.

The 575M Maranello was modified in subsequent years, first in 2004 with an enhanced Handling GTC package, with a stiffened suspension structure and motorsports-based suspension that the driver could adjust for Comfort or Sport, and then, in 2005, with the Superamerica, a 575M Maranello with a retractable hardtop.

Did You Know?

The 575 Maranello Handling GTC featured large 19-inch wheels through which you could see carbon-fiber brake discs, a feature previously seen only on the Ferrari Enzo.

As if the Ferrari Enzo wasn't exotic enough, late in the spring of 2004, Ferrari announced a track-only version of the car, the FXX, with only 29 units as an intended production run (though 30 were eventually produced).

The car was designed for what Ferrari termed Client Test Drivers, longtime and faithful Ferrari enthusiasts who might be capable of driving a car with 800 horsepower.

The FXX not only was equipped with 800 horsepower but with racing-derived telemetrics so FXX buyers could compare their lap times, throttle control, braking points, and some

FXX

Years produced: 2004–2007
Number produced: 30
Price: $2.1 million
Engine (displacement/horsepower): 6.3 liter V12/800 horsepower
0–60 miles per hour: 2.5 seconds
Top speed: 240 miles per hour

three dozen other parameters with those posted by the likes of Michael Schumacher, Rubens Barrichello, and other Ferrari F1 and professional development drivers. Customers

got bragging rights; Ferrari got real-world, albeit racetrack, data that it can use in designing future supercars that meet the needs of its best customers.

Power for the FXX comes from a 6.3-liter V12 that provides 800 horsepower at 8,500 rpm. A transmission derived from Formula One racing changes gears in less than 100 milliseconds. The FXX not only is more powerful than a 660-horsepower Enzo, it has 40 percent more downforce, and the car's rear spoiler can be adjusted to the demands of a specific track configuration.

Ferrari worked with Brembo to enhance the FXX's ceramic braking system and with Bridgestone on FXX-specific tires.

Did You Know?

FXX buyers were screened by a special committee, and after buying their cars—for some $2 million each—were promised invitations for the ensuing two years to a series of on-track driving experiences with the Ferrari racing team at various circuits.

For 2004, Ferrari was ready to replace the 360 Modena with an updated model, the F430 Berlinetta. But this really was much more than an updated model, even though some 30 percent—including the doors, hood, and roof—carried over from the previous car.

The F430 benefited from advances made by Ferrari when it was developing the Enzo and from technology transfer from the Formula One racing program.

Among the changes were a more rigid aluminum space frame, revised suspension,

F430 BERLINETTA

Years produced: 2004–2009
Number produced: Not available
Price: $169,000
Engine (displacement/horsepower): 4.3-liter V-8/490 horsepower
0–60 miles per hour: 4.0 seconds
Top speed: 196 miles per hour

speed-sensitive steering, carbon-fiber brakes, and especially E-Diff, an electronically controlled differential with five settings and

controlled by a steering wheel–mounted dial with settings for snow, slippery, sport, race, and disengage, each developed to enhance traction and control for varying road (or racetrack) conditions.

Also new was a body design that featured a front end inspired by the so-called shark-nose Grand Prix cars of the 1960s with twin rear air inlets on either side of the F430, one in the rocker area just ahead of the rear wheel and the other atop the rear fender. At the tail was a quartet of aerodynamic air diffusers.

Powering the F430 was a 4.3-liter V-8 enhanced with technology from the Enzo's V12. The result was 490 horsepower and nearly 350 lb-ft of torque, controlled by either a six-speed manual or paddle-shifted gearbox.

Did You Know?

An F430-based car with unique bodywork and feature, the Ferrari SP1 (Special Project Number 1), was designed through a new Ferrari Portfolio Program by Leonardo Fioravanti for Japanese businessman Junichiro Hiramatsu. The SP1 was declared the best-in-show at the 2010 Concorso Italiano, an Italian car concours held each summer at Monterey, California.

Modena. Enzo. Maranello. Ferrari became fond of naming its cars for places and people who were important to the company's history, and thus the logic behind the new 2+2 coupe for the 2004 model year, the 612 Scaglietti.

The name, of course, was a tribute to Sergio Scaglietti, the so-called "maestro of aluminum," whose small coachbuilding business was across the street from Ferrari's facility in the early days and therein created the bodywork for early Ferraris, especially for racing cars, including the famed 250 Testa Rossas.

612 SCAGLIETTI

Years produced: 2004–present
Number produced: Still in production
Price: $265,000
Engine (displacement/horsepower): 5.7-liter V12/540 horsepower
0–60 miles per hour: 4.2 seconds
Top speed: 170 miles per hour

Ferrari worked with aluminum manufacturer Alcoa on the engineering of the alloy space frame chassis that underlies this 2+2 coupe,

which represents Ferrari's first use of an all-aluminum vehicle with a V12 engine. The use of so much aluminum makes the car strong but light.

The engine in the 612 Scaglietti is a 5.7-liter unit evolved from the 575M Maranello and rated at 540 horsepower and capable of moving the four-seater at speeds of 170 miles per hour.

The 612 Scaglietti's wheelbase is longer than that of a Chevrolet Tahoe sport utility, which provides room inside for a degree of comfort for those sitting in the 2+2 seats.

In fact, the Scaglietti is the largest Ferrari of all, again a feature designed to provide room not only for a 12-cylinder engine but for four adults.

Did You Know?

The 612 designation for the engine in the Ferrari 612 Scaglietti also paid homage to Ferrari's history, specifically to the 612 sports racer (so called because of its 6.2-liter, 12-cylinder engine) that competed in the Canadian-American Challenge Cup—Can-Am—series in the late 1960s.

If you took only a quick glance at it parked with its top down, you might think the Superamerica was nothing more than a 575M Maranello convertible. And while the Superamerica was based on the 575M Maranello but provided an open cockpit, its roof system was innovative, though designed by someone with a long history in Ferrari design.

At Geneva in 2001, designer Leonardo Fioravanti presented his Vola concept, an enclosed roadster with a hardtop roof that rotated out of the way to a position immediately over the rear deck lid. Fioravanti's idea was to simplify increasingly complicated convertible tops and retractable roofs that

SUPERAMERICA

Years produced: 2005–2006
Number produced: 559
Price: Not available
Engine (displacement/horsepower): 5.8-liter V12/540 horsepower
0–60 miles per hour: 4.2 seconds
Top speed: 198 miles per hour

folded themselves up and disappeared into a compartment made available by an equally complex trunk lid that lifted itself out of the way so various motors could stow the top.

Fioravanti likes elegant simplicity. In 1996, he did a concept—NYCE—that featured such things as door panels that could fit either side of the vehicle, thus saving money and time in construction.

In his youth, Fioravanti had worked for Pininfarina, where he designed eight Ferrari models, including the Dino and Daytona. He later became design director at Ferrari, then opened his own design firm.

The roof of the Superamerica was based on Fioravanti's concept and used special electrochromic glass that could adjust the amount of light entering the cockpit, or could simply pivot out of the way to provide a full open-air driving experience.

Did You Know?

Based on the 575M Maranello, the Superamerica was among the world's fastest convertibles, capable of speeds just shy of 200 miles per hour.

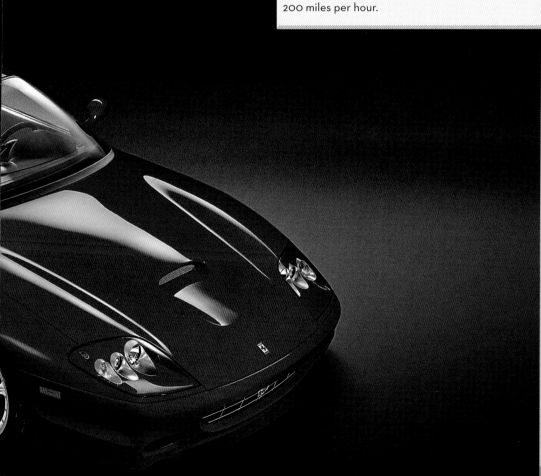

Making its debut at Geneva in 2006 was the successor to the 575M Maranello as Ferrari's premier front-engine, two-seat grand touring coupe. The name of the F599 GTB Fiorano comes from the car's engine displacement (5,999 cubic centimeters) and Ferrari's famed test track.

The 599 Fiorano's engine is based on the engine in the Ferrari Enzo, though with modifications so it will fit under the car's hood. The 6.0-liter V12 is rated at 620 horsepower, the highest figure yet for a Ferrari road car and enough power to propel the 599 Fiorano to speeds in excess of 200 miles per hour.

To further enhance the car's dynamic capability, a HGTE version, short for Handling Grand Touring Evolution, lowers the ride, stiffens the suspension, changes wheels and tires, alters the electronic controls for the transmission and engine, allows a more vocal exhaust, and updates the car inside and out with components made from carbon fiber.

At Geneva in 2009, Ferrari showed a 599XX model rated at 720 horsepower and designed only for use on closed racing circuits. Then, early in 2010, Ferrari said it also would create a 599 GTO that would be the company's fastest-ever street-legal automobile and that a 599 GTO prototype also had lapped the Fiorano track a second faster than the rear-engine Enzo. Ferrari also said only 599 of the new 599 GTOs will be built.

F599 GTB FIORANO

Years produced: 2006–present
Number produced: Still in production
Price: $327,000
Engine (displacement/horsepower): 6.0-liter V12/620 horsepower
0–60 miles per hour: 3.6 seconds
Top speed: 205 miles per hour

Did You Know?

At the fall 2010 Paris show, Ferrari presented the SA Aperta, a Targa-topped 599 GTO of which only 80 will be built in honor of the 80th anniversary of carrozzeria Pininfarina. The S and A in the car's name stand for Sergio and Andrea Pininfarina, son and grandson of company founder Battista "Pinin" Farina. *Aperta* is Italian for "open."

Unveiled at Paris in 2008, Ferrari showed the California, a 2+2 coupe with a retracting hardtop.

The California marked an additional model to the Ferrari lineup and also represented a number of "firsts" for Ferrari. It was the first Ferrari grand touring car using a front-mid placement for a V-8 engine. It was the first Ferrari with a retractable hard top. It was the first Ferrari with a seven-speed dual-clutch gearbox. It was the first Ferrari with a multi-link rear suspension. It was the first Ferrari with a direct-injection engine.

CALIFORNIA

Years produced: 2009–present
Number produced: Still in production
Price: $250,000
Engine (displacement/horsepower): 4.3-liter V-8/460 horsepower
0–60 miles per hour: 3.9 seconds
Top speed: 190 miles per hour

There also have been reports that the California will be the last Ferrari built with a clutch pedal and manual shifter and that all

future Ferraris will be shifted automatically or by paddles on the steering wheel without the need of a third pedal.

Pininfarina and Ferrari began design and engineering of the car in 2005. The styling features what Pininfarina calls a "nerve" or "stretched tendon" that tapers rearward from the air vents in the front fenders. This visual feature is designed to unify the car's sleek front end with a rear end that had to be large enough to house the retracted roof and the motors needed for it and the trunk lid to do

their ballet-like maneuvers when opening or closing the top.

Did You Know?

Tractor manufacturer Ferruccio Lamborghini complained to Enzo Ferrari about the 250 GT he'd purchased. Ferrari told him to go ahead and build his own if he thought he could make a better car. And thus was born the rival Italian sports car company. Ferrari also "inspired" Henry Ford II and Carroll Shelby to some of their greatest racing successes.

The Ferrari 458 Italia was introduced in the fall of 2009 at the Frankfurt Motor Show, and while it is the latest in a long line of mid-placed, V-8–powered Ferraris, Ferrari contends the car represents an "extreme" generational advancement in the 360 Modena/F430 heritage.

For one thing, the engine is the most powerful Ferrari has built for public roads. The all-new 4.5-liter powerplant offers 562 horsepower, spins to 9,000 rpm, and provides 398 lb-ft of torque.

F458 ITALIA

Years produced: 2010–present
Number produced: Still in production
Price: $230,000
Engine (displacement/horsepower): 4.5-liter V-8/562 horsepower
0–60 miles per hour: 3.4 seconds
Top speed: 202 miles per hour

The engine is linked to a seven-speed Formula One–style gearbox that can be paddle-shifted or will simply shift for itself.

Either way, it's a rocket ride—stop sign to 60 miles per hour in slightly more than three seconds. Keep your foot down and don't run out of pavement and the F458 Italia will top 200 miles per hour.

As in a Ferrari Grand Prix racer, the driver's controls—including the (third-generation) E-Diff and F1-Trac—are mounted on the steering wheel.

Like the engine, the steering, suspension, and chassis are new and designed to be strong but light.

The body, as usual designed by Pininfarina and the wind tunnel, is clean and devoid of add-ons but is full of subtle yet crucial elements, such as the placement of its air vents, front wings that adjust to enhance high-speed performance, and a tail treatment that provides not-so-subtle clues to the car's powerful nature with diffusers and central exhaust.

Did You Know?

The first Ferrari 458 Italia sold in the United States was auctioned to raise money for Haitian relief after the earthquake in 2009. The car brought $530,000—more than double its suggested retail price.

MARCHAL

INDEX